National Transportation Safety Board
Fiscal Year 2011 and 2010
Performance and Accountability Report

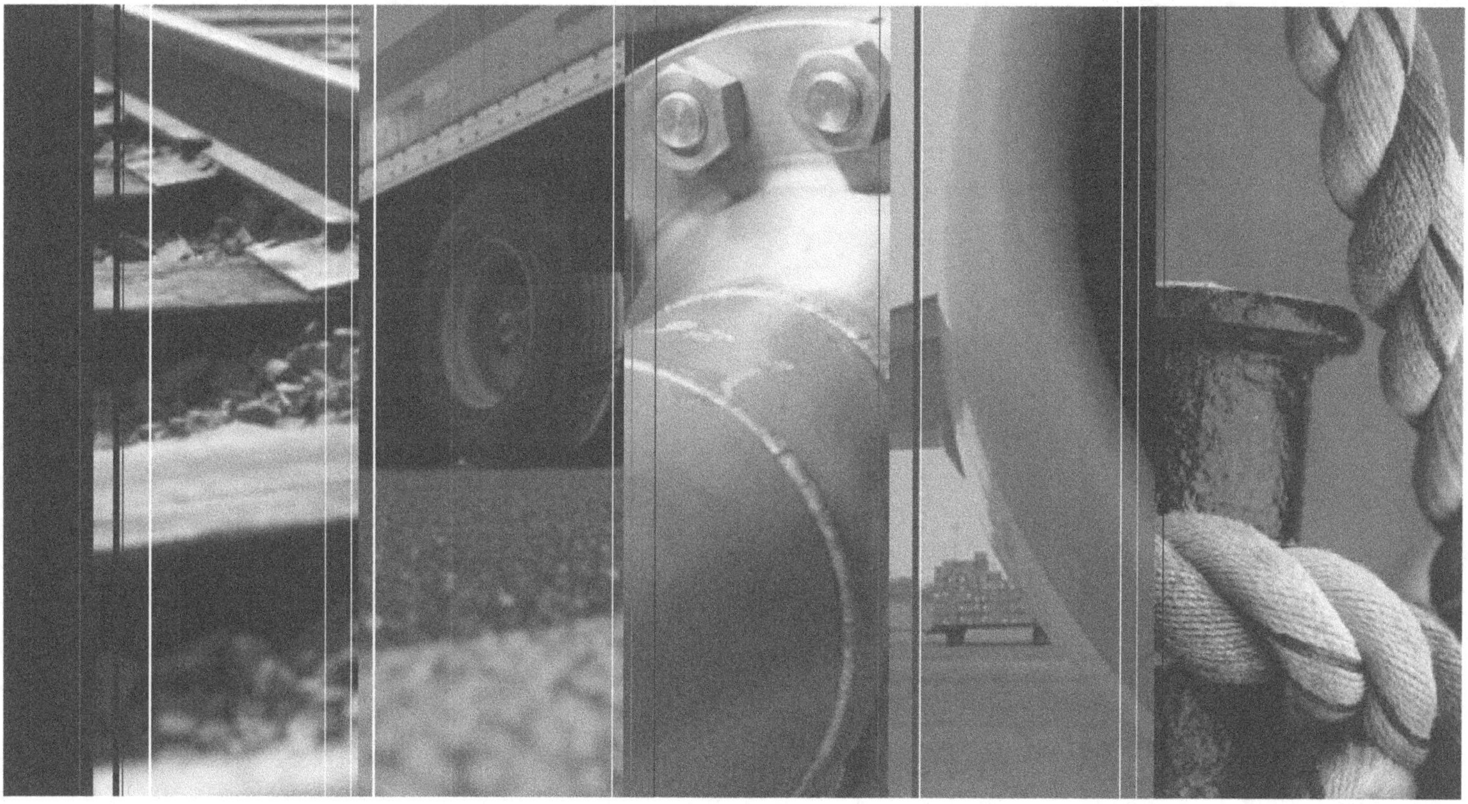

National
Transportation
Safety Board

THE NATIONAL TRANSPORTATION SAFETY BOARD AT A GLANCE

Established, April 1, 1967

Headquarters

490 L'Enfant Plaza, SW
Washington, DC 20594
www.ntsb.gov

FY 2011 Budget $98 million

FTE Employees, 405

How To Use This Report

This Performance and Accountability Report (PAR) for fiscal year (FY) 2011 and 2010 provides the National Transportation Safety Board (NTSB) financial and performance information that enables the President, Congress, and the American people to assess the agency's performance as provided by the requirements of the following legislation:

- Accountability of Tax Dollars Act of 2002
- Government Management Reform Act of 1994
- Government Performance and Results Act (GPRA) of 1993
- Chief Financial Officers Act of 1990
- Federal Manager's Financial Integrity Act (FMFIA) of 1982
- Office of Management and Budget (OMB) Circular A-136

This report compares performance results to the agency's strategic and performance goals. The NTSB's Strategic Plan and annual PARs are available on the NTSB's website at <http://www.ntsb.gov>. The NTSB welcomes feedback on the form and content of this report.

This report is organized as follows:

1. Letter from the Chairman

This includes an assessment of the reliability and completeness of the financial and performance information presented in the report and a statement of assurance of the agency's management controls as required by the FMFIA.

2. Management's Discussion and Analysis (MD&A)

This section provides an overview of the financial and performance information contained in the Performance and Financial Sections and Appendices. The MD&A includes an overview of the NTSB organization, highlights of the agency's performance goals and results, the current status of systems and internal control weaknesses, and other pertinent information, such as the progress being made by the NTSB in the President's Management Agenda.

3. Performance Section

This section provides annual performance information as required by OMB Circular A-11 and the GPRA and includes a detailed discussion and analysis of the agency's performance in FY 2011. It also includes information about past results of key performance measures.

4. Financial Section

This section contains details of the NTSB's FY 2011 finances and includes the Office of the Inspector General (OIG) Quality Control Report, the Independent Auditor's Report, the NTSB Chief Financial Officer's (CFO) Response to the Auditor's Report, the agency's audited financial statements and notes to the financial statements.

Mission Statement

To promote transportation safety by:

- maintaining our congressionally mandated independence and objectivity;
- conducting objective, precise accident investigations and safety studies;
- performing fair and objective airman and mariner certification appeals; and
- advocating and promoting NTSB safety recommendations. And to assist victims of transportation accidents and their families.

Strategic Goals

Strategic Goal #1 - Accomplish Objective Investigations of Transportation Accidents to Identify Issues and Actions that Improve Transportation Safety

Strategic Goal #2 – Increase our Impact on the Safety of the Transportation System

Strategic Goal #3 – Outstanding Stewardship of Resources

Strategic Goal #4 – Organizational Excellence

Table of Contents

The NTSB's Vital Role in Transportation Safety

Since its creation in 1967 as an accident investigation agency within the newly created U.S. Department of Transportation (DOT), the NTSB's mission has been to determine the probable cause of transportation accidents and to formulate safety recommendations to improve transportation safety. The NTSB's authority currently extends to the following:

- All U.S. civil aviation accidents and certain public-use aircraft accidents;
- Selected highway accidents;
- Railroad accidents involving passenger trains or selected freight train accidents that result in fatalities or significant property damage;
- Major marine accidents and any marine accident involving both a public and a nonpublic vessel;
- Pipeline accidents involving fatalities, substantial property damage, or significant environmental damage;
- Selected accidents resulting in the release of hazardous materials in any mode of transportation; and
- Selected transportation accidents that involve problems of a recurring nature or that are catastrophic.

In 1974, Congress passed the Independent Safety Board Act, which severed the NTSB's ties to the DOT and authorized the agency to do the following:

- Evaluate the effectiveness of government agencies involved in transportation safety;
- Evaluate the safeguards used in the transportation of hazardous materials;
- Evaluate the effectiveness of emergency responses to hazardous material accidents;
- Conduct special studies on safety problems;
- Maintain official U.S. census of aviation accidents;
- Review appeals from airmen, mechanics, and repairmen who have been assessed civil penalties by the Federal Aviation Administration (FAA); and
- Review appeals from airmen and merchant seamen whose certificates have been revoked or suspended.

The NTSB also leads U.S. teams assisting in foreign airline accident investigations conducted by foreign authorities under the provisions of International Civil Aviation Organization (ICAO) agreements. In 1996, the Aviation Disaster Family Assistance Act further assigned to the NTSB the responsibility of coordinating Federal Government resources and other organizations to support the efforts of local and state authorities and the airlines in assisting aviation disaster victims and their families following accidents in which there is a major loss of life. A subsequent Presidential memorandum directed

Federal agencies to support the NTSB when it assumes the same responsibilities for major surface transportation accidents. The Rail Passenger Disaster Family Assistance Act of 2008 assigned similar responsibilities to the NTSB for rail passenger disasters resulting in a major loss of life, regardless of the cause or suspected cause.

To date, the NTSB has investigated more than 140,000 aviation accidents and thousands of surface transportation accidents. On call 24 hours a day, 365 days a year, NTSB investigators have traveled throughout the country and to every corner of the world to perform investigations. Thanks to this dedication, the NTSB is recognized as the world's leading accident investigation agency.

More than 13,000 safety recommendations have been issued to more than 2,500 recipients in all transportation modes as a result of NTSB investigations. Since 1990, the NTSB has published a "Most Wanted" list of transportation safety improvements, which highlights safety-critical actions that the DOT modal administrations, the U.S. Coast Guard (USCG), and the states need to take to help prevent accidents and save lives. The NTSB does not have authority to regulate transportation equipment, personnel or operations, or to initiate enforcement action. However, based on its reputation for objectivity and thoroughness, the NTSB has achieved such success in shaping transportation safety improvements that those who are in a position to effect these changes have accepted more than 82 percent of the agency's recommendations. Many safety features currently incorporated into airplanes, automobiles, trains, pipelines, and marine vessels had their genesis in these recommendations.

The NTSB meets its important safety mission through several lines of business that work together to prevent future accidents. These lines of business are:

The Office of Aviation Safety (AS): The mission of AS is to investigate all air carriers, commuter and air taxi accidents, in-flight collisions, fatal and nonfatal general aviation accidents, and certain public-use aircraft accidents; to participate in the investigation of major airline crashes in foreign countries that involve U.S. carriers or U.S.-manufactured or -designed equipment to fulfill U.S. obligations under International Civil Aviation Organizational agreements; and to conduct investigations of safety issues that extend beyond a single accident to examine specific aviation safety problems from a broader perspective. AS conducts investigation activities through six specialty divisions: Major Investigations, Aviation Engineering, Operational Factors, Human Performance and Survival Factors, Writing and Editing, and Regional Offices. The regional investigation management structure in AS consists of 4 regions with 10 regional offices. International aviation coordination is staffed within the immediate office of the Director of AS.

The Office of Highway Safety (HS): HS investigates those accidents that have a significant impact on the public's confidence in highway transportation safety, that generate high public interest and media attention, or that highlight national safety issues, such as collapses of highway bridge structures, fatalities on public transportation vehicles (such as buses and vans), and collisions at highway/rail grade crossings. In addition, HS conducts studies based on trends emerging from NTSB accident investigations and from other research and accident data to identify common risks or underlying causes of accidents. To accomplish these tasks, HS includes the Investigations Division and the Report Development Division.

The Office of Marine Safety (MS): MS investigates major marine accidents on navigable waters of the United States, accidents involving U.S. merchant vessels in international waters, collisions involving U.S. public and nonpublic vessels, and select marine accidents that involve public transportation or those of a recurring nature. The USCG conducts the preliminary investigation of all marine accidents and notifies the NTSB if an accident is a major marine accident. Once such contact is made, the NTSB conducts an independent investigation, participates in a joint NTSB/USCG investigation, or requests the USCG to conduct an investigation on behalf of the NTSB. MS is organized into three Investigations Divisions.

The Office of Railroad, Pipeline and Hazardous Materials Investigations (RPH): RPH investigates accidents involving railroads, pipelines, and the transportation of hazardous materials. On the basis of the investigations conducted by this office, the NTSB issues safety recommendations to Federal and state regulatory agencies, industry and safety standards organizations, carriers and pipeline operators, equipment and container manufactures, producers and shippers of hazardous materials, and emergency response organizations. RPH consists of four divisions: Railroad, Pipeline and Hazardous Materials, Human Performance and Survival Factors, and Report Development.

The Office of Research and Engineering (RE): RE provides technical support to accident investigations and conducts safety studies that examine safety issues in all modes of transportation. The NTSB's Flight Data Recorder, Cockpit Voice Recorder, and Materials Laboratories are located in this office. The office also provides periodic statistical reviews of aviation accidents.

The Office of Communications (OC): OC includes four divisions: Advocacy, Public Affairs, Government Affairs, and Transportation Disaster Assistance (TDA). The mission of OC is to ensure that the NTSB's vision and actions are accurately and effectively communicated to congressional stakeholders, victims of transportation accidents and their families, state and local governments, the press, and the public, resulting in successful understanding of the NTSB mission and implementation of actions on critical transportation safety issues.

The NTSB's Most Wanted List of Transportation Safety Improvements, administered by the Office of Communications, highlights recommendations that would have the greatest impact on transportation safety at the national and state levels. Although the NTSB actively advocates for the acceptance of all of its recommendations, follow up efforts for the recommendations on the Most Wanted List are generally more aggressive.

The Office of Administration (AD): AD coordinates and manages the infrastructure and support activities for the agency. This office provides human resource management, labor relations, facilities management, safety, security, and acquisitions and lease management. Physical inventory, shipping and receiving, telecommunications, and management of the NTSB's hearing room and conference center are also major functions managed by this office. Work is carried out in three divisions: Facilities Operations, Human Resources, and Acquisition and Lease Management.

The Office of Administrative Law Judges (ALJ): ALJ serves as the "court of appeals" for airmen and mariners facing the loss or suspension of their licensing certificates, or the imposition of a civil penalty.

The Office of the Chief Information Officer (CIO): CIO provides strategic direction and operation support for the NTSB's information systems, and develops and distributes programs and products for use by the NTSB and the public. CIO consists of five divisions: Computer Services, Systems Support, Records Management, Information Security, and Enterprise Architect.

The Office of the Chief Financial Officer (CFO): CFO manages the NTSB financial resources, develops the agency's budget requests for submission to the Office of Management and Budget and to Congress, and executes the budget for resources appropriated to the NTSB by Congress. CFO also prepares the agency financial statements required by the Accountability of Tax Dollars Act, oversees the agency property and inventory control programs, and analyzes the fee structure for services that the agency provides on a reimbursable basis. Additionally, CFO is responsible for ensuring the NTSB's compliance with the Federal Manager's Financial Integrity Act. CFO consists of the Budget and Planning Division and the Financial Analysis and Reporting Division.

The Office of General Counsel (GC): GC advises, assists, and represents the NTSB in support of its activities. As the legal advisor to the NTSB, it is responsible for determining legal policy for the agency.

The Office of the Managing Director (MD): The MD provides overall leadership for the management of the agency, including production, strategy, and support functions. MD ensures that NTSB resources are allocated appropriately so that the NTSB performs its mission to promote transportation safety in the most cost-effective manner.

MD includes the Safety Recommendations and Quality Assurance Division and the NTSB Training Center. Safety recommendations are the NTSB's most important products and are the foundation of the agency's accident-prevention role. Issued to government agencies at all levels, transportation operators, safety organizations, and other key transportation stakeholders, safety recommendations are used to bring about improvements to the nation's transportation system. The NTSB's recommendations are not mandatory, but, to emphasize their importance, Congress requires the DOT and its agencies to respond to recommendations within 90 days of their issuance.

The NTSB Training Center: The NTSB Training Center is responsible for internal staff training, training plans, and workforce development programs. The Training Center, located in Ashburn, Virginia, provides training opportunities for all NTSB employees and others from the transportation community through a variety of course offerings. The core curriculum has been and continues to be key investigative courses that focus on competencies important to safety investigations.

A Message from the Chairman

I am pleased to present the FY 2011 Annual Performance and Accountability Report for the NTSB. This report details the agency's accomplishments and challenges in upholding our mission to promote transportation safety; it is also an accounting to the American people of our stewardship of the funding we received from them in FY 2011 to fulfill our mission. This report contains the NTSB's financial statements, as required by OMB Circular A-136, a selection of annual performance information, and a report on the NTSB's internal controls, as required by the FMFIA.

The NTSB is recognized internationally for its aviation accident investigation expertise. The same tenacity and dedication to excellence are applied to accident investigations in all other modes of transportation. For over 40 years, the NTSB has been at the forefront of transportation safety issues—the conscience, if you will, of America's vital transportation network. The NTSB not only constitutes our nation's premier accident investigation agency, but also enjoys an excellent reputation as the most authoritative independent safety investigative body in the world. The NTSB's dedicated staff has worked long and hard over the years to maintain its reputation as being the "best in the safety business."

The NTSB's FY 2002 financial statements were the first such documents in the history of the agency. Building on this valuable experience and accomplishment, since FY 2003 the NTSB has achieved nine consecutive unqualified (clean) opinions on our audited consolidated financial statements.

Leon Snead & Company, P.C., an independent public accounting firm engaged by the Department of Transportation Office of Inspector General (DOT-IG), has audited the NTSB's FY 2011 consolidated financial statements included in this report and has issued an unqualified (clean) opinion indicating that our statements present fairly the financial position of the NTSB. This is the best possible audit result and affirms our commitment to financial reporting excellence.

Along with this opinion, I am pleased to report on the NTSB's compliance with the FMFIA and revised OMB Circular A-123, "Management's Responsibility for Internal Control" for September 30, 2011. The FMFIA requires the NTSB to annually evaluate its management controls and identify any material weaknesses. This requirement covers all of the agency's programs and administrative functions. As we work to serve the American people, we must administer our programs as efficiently and economically as possible. To do this, we rely on our system of management controls to provide reasonable assurance that our financial activities comply with applicable laws, our items of value are safeguarded, and our operations are accounted for properly.

As of September 30, 2011, there is no new material weakness to report. In addition, the NTSB has fully implemented or made significant progress in adopting leading management practices in all areas where the Government Accounting Office made prior recommendations. These areas include (1) communication, strategic planning, information technology, knowledge management, organizational structure, human capital management, training, and financial management; (2) increasing the efficiency of activities related to investigating accidents, issuing recommendations, and conducting safety studies; and (3) increasing the use of our Training Center.

The selected performance goals contained in this report summarize our success in achieving the performance goals we established for FY 2011. The NTSB continues to aggressively improve our performance planning practices to ensure that, in the future, our goals are results driven and oriented toward achieving desired outcomes.

Just as the NTSB is the world's premier accident investigation agency, it is our vision that we become a premier financial management agency in the Federal government. The submission of our Performance and Accountability Report is another step toward that vision.

Sincerely,

/s/

Deborah A.P. Hersman
Chairman

From The Chief Financial Officer

I am pleased to report that during fiscal year 2011 the National Transportation Safety Board (NTSB) continued to honor its commitment to lead by example in government financial management. For the ninth consecutive year, since being required to prepare audited financial statements, our independent auditors presented NTSB with an unqualified (clean) opinion on our financial statements, citing no new material weakness and no major compliance problems.

The financial statements that follow were prepared, audited, and made publicly available as an integral part of this performance and accountability report (PAR). These financial statements fairly present the NTSB's financial position and were prepared in accordance with generally accepted accounting principles in the United States of America and the Office of Management and Budget.

In fiscal year FY 2011, the NTSB continued its efforts toward organizational excellence, which is defined by results. Progress for much of our efforts toward excellence is captured in the NTSB FY 2011 and 2010 Performance and Accountability Report. The report provides the NTSB's most important financial and performance information. It is also our principal publication and report to Congress and the American people on our program leadership and our stewardship and management of the public funds entrusted to us.

With the attainment of the independent's auditor's unqualified financial statement opinion, the Office of the Chief Financial Officer is committed to moving forward vigorously during FY 2012 to continue improving our internal control processes and fulfilling our financial management improvement goals.

Steven E. Goldberg
November 1, 2011

Management's Discussion & Analysis

Overview

Since its creation in 1967 as an independent accident investigation agency within the newly created U.S. Department of Transportation (DOT), the NTSB's mission has been to determine the probable cause of transportation accidents and to formulate safety recommendations to improve transportation safety. The NTSB's authority currently extends to the following:

- All U.S. civil aviation accidents and certain public-use aircraft accidents;
- Selected highway accidents;
- Railroad accidents involving passenger trains or selected freight train accidents that result in fatalities or significant property damage;
- Major marine accidents and any marine accident involving both a public and a nonpublic vessel;
- Pipeline accidents involving fatalities, substantial property damage, or significant environmental damage;
- Selected accidents resulting in the release of hazardous materials in any mode of transportation; and
- Selected transportation accidents that involve problems of a recurring nature or that are catastrophic.

In 1974, Congress passed the Independent Safety Board Act, which severed the NTSB's ties to the DOT and authorized the agency to do the following:

- Evaluate the effectiveness of government agencies involved in transportation safety;
- Evaluate the safeguards used in the transportation of hazardous materials;
- Evaluate the effectiveness of emergency responses to hazardous material accidents;
- Conduct special studies on safety problems;
- Maintain official U.S. census of aviation accidents;
- Review appeals from airmen, mechanics, and repairmen who have been assessed civil penalties by the FAA; and
- Review appeals from airmen and merchant seamen whose certificates have been revoked or suspended.

History and Structure of the NTSB

The NTSB opened its doors on April 1, 1967, initially relying on the DOT for funding and administrative support. Although its charter is the Independent Safety Board Act of 1974, the origins of the NTSB can be found in the Air Commerce Act of 1926, in which Congress charged the Commerce Department with investigating the causes of aircraft accidents. The rules of the NTSB are located in Chapter VIII, Title 49 of the Code of Federal Regulations.

The five-member Board is composed of appointees nominated by the President and confirmed by the Senate. A Chairman (who is designated by the President and subject to a separate Senate confirmation) serves as the chief executive officer of the NTSB. The President also designates one of the Members as Vice Chairman.

The NTSB's headquarters office is located in Washington, DC. The NTSB also has regional offices in Ashburn, Virginia; Atlanta, Georgia; Miami, Florida; West Chicago, Illinois; Arlington, Texas; Denver, Colorado; Anchorage, Alaska; Seattle, Washington; and Gardena, California. The Office of Aviation Safety has reorganized the staff assigned to offices in the 48 contiguous states into three mega-regional offices; Alaska constitutes the fourth region. In addition, two aviation investigators are based in Hawaii. The following chart depicts the major organizational components, reporting relationships, and budget program structure of the NTSB.

National Transportation Safety Board

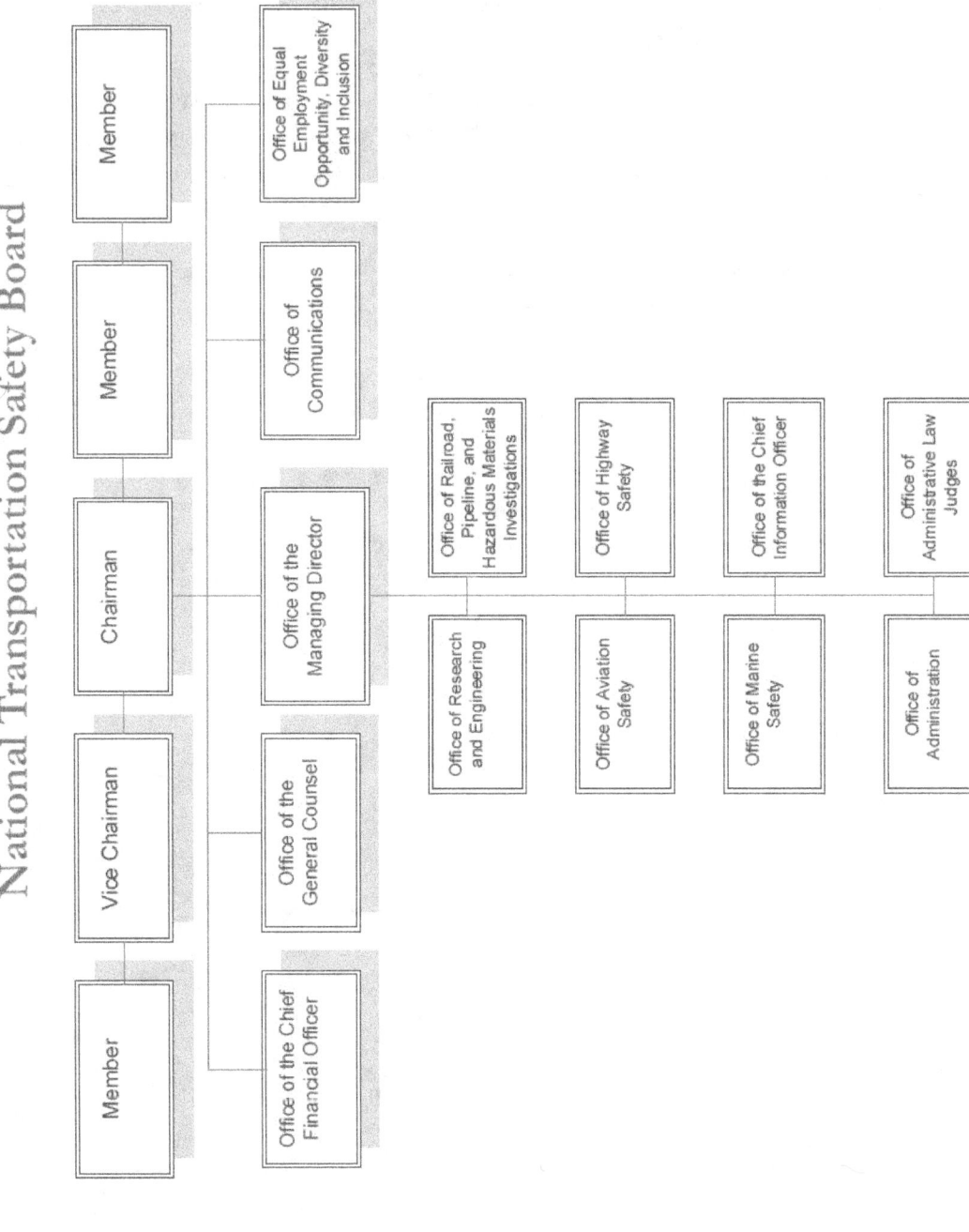

The Board consists of five Members appointed by the President with the advice and consent of the Senate. The President appoints the Chairman and Vice Chairman for 2-year terms. The Chairman is additionally confirmed by the Senate, and serves as the agency chief executive and administrative officer. The Board Members, in conjunction with the Chairman, establish policies on transportation safety issues; review and approve major accident reports, safety studies, and safety recommendations; and decide appeals of NTSB Administrative Law Judge initial decisions regarding Federal Aviation Administration and Coast Guard certificate actions. They also preside over accident or other transportation safety hearings, testify before Congressional committees, and participate in go-teams on major investigations.

Independence

The NTSB's status as an independent government agency makes it different from other stakeholders in the transportation industry. Transportation companies are motivated by financial gain, and many are ultimately accountable to their shareholders. Other government agencies (for example, the FAA, the Federal Railroad Administration, the Federal Highway Administration, and the U.S. Coast Guard), have an official role in establishing and enforcing industry regulations. The NTSB has no such interests or obligations. Our most important stakeholder is the traveling public, and we are concerned with one thing: promoting transportation safety for the traveling public.

Investigations

NTSB staff takes an unbiased approach to each accident that the agency investigates. Local authorities, industry representatives, and other agencies are frequently called upon to participate as parties to the NTSB's investigations. Our only objective is to determine the probable cause of the accident and to extract lessons learned that will prevent similar accidents in the future. The NTSB's reputation as an honest broker is an important reason why state and local governments, Federal agencies, and even foreign countries welcome and encourage the NTSB to lead important accident investigations.

Actions to correct deficiencies that contribute to accidents are often identified early in the investigative process. The NTSB strongly supports and encourages voluntary efforts to effect safety changes and works with parties to implement such changes. In other situations, the NTSB invokes a more formal process of issuing safety recommendations, which ask government agencies, parties to the investigation, or other entities to take action to improve safety. Some of these recommendations are made during the accident investigation. In other cases, the NTSB makes safety recommendations at the conclusion of the investigative process and incorporates them into the official accident reports.

Performance Section

Strategic Goals and Strategic Objectives

Strategic Goal #1 – Accomplish Objective Investigations of Transportation Accidents

Summary

Strategic Goal 1 reflects the core mission of the NTSB and is divided into the following strategic objectives:

- Make judicious selections of accidents to investigate in each transportation mode;

- Appropriately scale the investigative response to accidents;

- Develop and maintain state-of-the-art investigative analytic and procedural tools for accident investigations; and

- Ensure effective coordination and delivery of Transportation Disaster Assistance to accident victims.

Although the respective performance of all NTSB offices can influence Strategic Goal 1, there is particular emphasis on the modal investigative offices to ensure this goal and its strategic objectives are met. This strategic goal focuses on the NTSB's key challenge to identify those accidents in each transportation mode that represent the most important targets of investigative opportunity and determine the appropriate scope and scale of such investigations. Accomplishing the strategic objectives for this goal will ensure effective and efficient investigation of transportation accidents and incidents and foster a transportation industry that is better prepared to address safety issues.

Key Management Issues and Challenges

The cost of transportation accidents to society is significant, and the growth in transportation system activity in the United States will intensify the problem. Accompanying this growth are enormous increases in the system's complexity, which must be addressed with techniques and methods of accident investigation that are equally complex. In order to conduct thorough accident investigations, NTSB investigators must stay abreast of the latest technology available in the transportation industry; this requires substantial and continuing training. The NTSB's challenge is to identify the available resources and staff to ensure and provide training in these areas. Another challenge is the difficulty in scheduling training due to the number and timing of accidents and the limited number of investigators. The number of major airline accidents worldwide has increased, and aviation safety staff participates in 19 major foreign accident investigations annually, on average. This participation presents a particular challenge since the office must also continue to meet its mandate to investigate all aviation accidents in the United States.

A key challenge for the NTSB is to identify those accidents in each transportation mode that represent the most important targets of investigative opportunity and to determine the appropriate scope and scale of such investigations. This selection process must balance the significance of the safety issues involved in these accidents against the limited investigative resources available to the NTSB and the depth of the investigation required to develop the safety issues. Overall, accomplishing objective accident investigations is a critical component of our mission, and it is done with transparency, accountability, and integrity—the core values of the agency's vision.

Strategic Objectives

1. Make Judicious Selections of Accidents to Investigate in Each Transportation Mode

The resources available to the NTSB do not permit us to investigate every accident in every mode. We will judiciously determine the significance of accidents and balance that against the level of investigative effort that would be necessary in each occurrence, which may mean, in some cases, not conducting an investigation. This selection process requires careful monitoring of accident events in each mode and a careful evaluation of safety issues by technical experts in each modal office. After this evaluation is complete, we will select accidents in which we launch on a case-by-case basis to ensure the maximum potential value for increasing transportation safety.

2. Appropriately Scale the Investigative Response to Accidents

We will evaluate and refine our ability to establish the proper scope of investigative activity and to respond appropriately during both the on-scene and follow-up phases of accident investigations. Included in these assessments will be a determination of the level of documentation and report development, including expedited report formats, required for each case. Based on this scaling, each investigation will result in an appropriate level of reporting and recommendations issued to promote positive safety outcomes.

3. Develop and Maintain State-of-the-Art Investigative and Procedural Tools for Accident Investigations

The nature of the NTSB's mission and mandate demands that the agency be operationally sophisticated and fully equipped to conduct increasingly complex investigations in the 21st century. We will refine and enhance investigative techniques and procedural tools that are integral to our accident investigations. We also will ensure that our investigators, engineers, and professionals are equipped with and trained to use new tools and techniques that will keep us on the cutting edge of investigation science and technology.

4. Ensure Effective Coordination and Delivery of Transportation Disaster Assistance to Accident Victims

In addition to our investigative response, the NTSB coordinates public and private support response in the wake of transportation disasters for all modes of transportation. The TDA team stands ready to help survivors, families of victims, communities, and commercial carriers deal with transportation disasters. TDA staff will provide an Incident Command Liaison (ICL) to efficiently coordinate the agency's response and investigation with the on-scene emergency response. An ICL will be sent for all major Aviation accidents and Rail accidents, as legislated, as well as other modes as needed. The launching of TDA staff to fulfill family assistance and victim identification duties frees on-scene accident investigators from handling these functions, thus providing a more efficient on-scene presence.2

Strategic Goal #2 – From Investigations, Recommend and Advocate Actions that will Improve Transportation Safety

Summary

Because the NTSB's mission is to promote transportation safety, Strategic Goal 2, which impacts the safety of the entire transportation system, cascades into strategic objectives that emphasize outreach and advocacy. Leveraging our unique position in the safety industry, the NTSB believes it is necessary to provide leadership to the transportation community and to ensure that emerging safety issues are being addressed and political leadership is aware of public policy implications. To achieve this goal, Strategic Goal 2 has the following objectives:

- Provide objective and independent advice on transportation safety issues;

- Engage in outreach with the transportation community to advance safety;

- Advocate the implementation of safety recommendations with emphasis on the Most Wanted List of Transportation Safety Improvements;

- Constructively affect the transportation industry;

- Improve our investigative readiness by identifying emerging safety issues; and

- Maintain a fair and expeditious appeals process for airmen and mariners.

In implementing these objectives, the agency informs and involves Congress in the NTSB's mission and promotes agreement by industry stakeholders on the most pressing safety issues in the transportation industry. Furthermore, this strategic goal emphasizes the need for the NTSB to promote an understanding of the Most Wanted List of Transportation Safety Improvements, in which we have identified areas of risk that can lead to additional accidents. Our planned actions include actively working with Congress, other government agencies, and industry groups to bring about a safer transportation system for the future, based on our current knowledge of safety issues. We also need to stay abreast of emerging safety issues so that our investigative readiness is never compromised. Moreover, safe transportation relies on qualified and licensed operators of aircraft and surface transportation vehicles. Consequently, this strategic goal includes a fair appeals process for airmen and mariners to ensure a thorough adjudication and to ensure that those licensed to operate in transportation modes carrying the American public possess the highest standards of safety and professionalism.

Key Management Issues and Challenges

The nation's level of transportation activity, which highly correlates with its level of economic activity, continues to increase. As our skies, highways, waterways, and railways become more congested, the potential for transportation accidents increases. With limited resources, the NTSB is challenged to identify ways to address implementation of its open safety recommendations. Another area of concern is increasing the NTSB's presence at sessions of state legislatures for the purpose of elevating the priority of highway safety at the state level and increasing legislators' understanding of the issues.

Finally, the length and complexity of the rulemaking process has resulted in Federal agencies frequently not acting to address NTSB recommendations in a timely fashion. The NTSB is challenged to ensure that the rulemaking process, which can take years, does not hamper the successful implementation of recommendations. Working with Congress, other government agencies, and industry groups, the NTSB takes an active role in leading efforts for a safer transportation system. During FY 2010, the NTSB, as requested, provided information supporting legislative and/or regulatory changes addressing state-related safety recommendations 23 times. The NTSB also issued 227 recommendations, including 170 aviation, 18 highway, 25 railroad, 7 marine and 7 pipeline recommendations. Over the last 5 years, the NTSB has issued 938 safety recommendations across all modes of transportation. During 2010, a total of 189 recommendations were closed. Safety recommendation acceptance rates for all modes of transportation remain consistent, with more than 80 percent of our recommendations being implemented.

Strategic Objectives

1. Provide Objective and Independent Advice on Transportation Safety Issues

We will use various approaches to work with Congress and congressional staff to advance important issues related to the NTSB's transportation safety mission, focusing on increasing their understanding of our core mission work and any other associated activities. We will use a number of approaches to accomplish this objective, including reaching out to individuals in person and publishing such reports as the NTSB Annual Report to Congress.

2. Engage in Outreach with the Transportation Community to Advance Safety

NTSB staff will continue to be active members of the transportation community to promote our recommendations and positions on safety issues. We will participate on technical committees and will speak at industry conferences to increase the community's understanding of safety issues, creating partnerships with stakeholders to improve safety. We will take special care to ensure that our activities associated with this strategy enhance our reputation as objective and thorough accident investigators. Finally, we will utilize the Internet to further engage with the transportation community and the traveling public.

3. Advocate the Implementation of Safety Recommendations with Emphasis on the Most Wanted List of Transportation Safety Improvements

Through advocacy activities at the Federal and state levels, we will press for the adoption of those recommendations that will have the most significant impact on improving transportation safety, including those included on our Most Wanted List of Transportation Safety Improvements.

We will undertake an initiative to focus on the most important safety issues—those with the greatest potential to save lives. We will develop an advocacy plan outlining a mix of public, congressional, governmental, and industry activities to increase implementation of recommendations for each issue included on the Most Wanted List. We will also continue our regular meetings with DOT modal agencies to work for implementation of all our open recommendations.

4. Constructively Affect the Transportation Industry

Through recommendations issued in accident reports, safety studies, and other products, the NTSB will provide concrete and timely advice to improve transportation safety. With almost 13,000 recommendations issued to date, the NTSB has contributed to significant results in all transportation modes, and, as a result, the American transportation industry is safer today than it has ever been. Our investigative process involves the development of factual records and safety recommendations with one aim—to ensure that accidents like the ones investigated never happen again. This strategic objective showcases the NTSB's proactive and constructive approach in achieving positive safety outcomes, with emphasis on legislative, regulatory, and enforcement action.

5. Improve Investigative Readiness by Identifying Emerging Safety Issues

To focus attention on important transportation safety issues, RE will continue to develop and update an Emerging Issues List. Distinct from the existing NTSB Most Wanted List of Transportation Safety Improvements, the Emerging Issues List tracks key safety issues, including those uncovered through accident investigations, outreach activities, and NTSB public forums. Each NTSB investigative office will contribute issues to the list annually.

6. Maintain a Fair and Expeditious Appeals Process for Airmen and Mariners

The NTSB serves as the "court of appeals" for airmen and mariners facing the loss or suspension of their licensing certificates or the imposition of a civil penalty. We will promote transportation safety by adjudicating airman appeals of certificate actions and denials, providing due process to those affected and ensuring the integrity of the aviation and maritime safety enforcement system. This strategic objective demonstrates NTSB values of integrity, objectivity, and thoroughness in our work.

Strategic Goal #3 – Outstanding Stewardship of Resources

Summary

The NTSB ensures that our limited dollars are used in the most efficient manner. With limited funding and approximately 405 employees, stewardship of resources must be outstanding. Therefore, Strategic Goal 3 cascades into the following specific strategic objectives:

- Employ project management best practices to maximize the effective use of agency resources while maintaining high quality;
- Effectively use the allocated funds to execute the mission; and
- Utilize effective information technology to accomplish the organization's mission.

Project planning principles are incorporated into all major efforts to achieve these objectives, promoting efficiency in major work-product outputs. The NTSB will increase our use of project management in all facets of our operations. This strategic goal focuses on the NTSB's efforts to efficiently use resources in a responsible and results-oriented manner while ensuring that the agency is able to fulfill our broad mission. We are committed to ensuring that the stewardship of resources—including the use of best practices in project planning, controlling costs, and deploying cost-effective technology—is reflected in the operating plans of all offices, both investigative and non-investigative. As the NTSB faces continuing challenges in meeting our mission in an environment of limited government resources, we will focus on office target levels to ensure that transportation safety remains of the highest importance while maintaining outstanding stewardship of resources.

Key Management Issues and Challenges

The NTSB has a duty to ensure that the resources appropriated to it by Congress are expended in an efficient, responsible, and results-oriented manner. A large component of NTSB expenses is personnel, and, as a result, we must accomplish our mission within the current staffing levels in spite of the fact that the scope of our responsibility is broad and our team of dedicated employees is relatively small. To meet this challenge, we have been using our resources efficiently and are taking steps to ensure that we continue to make the most efficient and effective use of our staff, budget, information technology, and other resources.

Strategic Objectives

1. Employ Project Management Best Practices to Maximize the Effective Use of Agency Resources While Maintaining High Quality

We will evaluate our major work products and processes to identify best practices and to eliminate inefficiencies. Major work products include accident investigation reports, public hearings, and complex administrative and information technology (IT) projects. To increase project efficiency, the centerpiece of this strategy will be project planning and all associated planned actions. Developing a project plan and post-project process assessment will be standard parts of every major work effort. This strategy will promote efficient deployment of the agency's personnel, budget, and other resources. The NTSB has been instituting project management throughout the agency by deploying project management tools and best practices, piloting a new efficient model for the accident investigative process, and implementing project management curriculum and training at the Training Center.

2. Effectively Use the Allocated Funds to Execute the Mission

We have continually focused on accomplishing the agency mission within budgetary constraints; this will continue in the future. CFO will ensure that offices are allocated funds in a timely manner. Within guidance provided for administrative control of funds, we will ensure that we develop spending plans that effectively use funds provided in office allocations. NTSB offices will monitor commitments to ensure timely processing and reconciliations of purchase card transactions. To ensure that resources are allocated to the highest and most urgent agency priorities, offices will submit proposals for resources that cannot be accommodated within initial allocations. Agency leadership will prioritize these proposals and provide decisions in a timely manner to facilitate reallocation of funds, including any necessary legal reviews. Offices also will ensure timely coordination with GC and CFO for all reimbursable agreements.

3. Utilize Effective Information Technology to Accomplish the Organization's Mission

We will continue to use Information Technology (IT) to effectively capture data and information electronically at the earliest possible point and to move data and information across the organization using sound business processes. Using a mixture of commercially available solutions and enhancements to in-house applications, we will deploy workflow solutions to improve the efficiency of operations in both modal and business support functions. We will work to address the changing nature of the Federal workforce and test, adopt, and implement technologies designed to empower a highly mobile workforce that works in a variety of locations (for example, on-scene, in the office, at home) and that is capable of sending and receiving information securely in electronic form with key constituents. Further, we will deploy software to transform how data and information are managed, shared, and used by both internal and external customers. NTSB stakeholders will have access to increasing amounts of data, information, and tools that will enhance our ability to identify trends, define key data relationships, and interact with a broad-based community on a wide variety of safety issues. Collectively, these efforts will leverage our ability to use IT as a key element in accomplishing the agency's mission.

Strategic Goal #4 – Organizational Excellence

Summary

The first three strategic goals are embodied in the fourth strategic goal, which captures the overall nature of the organization: excellence. Strategic Goal 4 is divided into the following objectives:

- Integrate long-range planning in all elements of NTSB business;
- Align and improve human capital planning;

- Maintain a competent and effective workforce through targeted training and employee development; and

- Foster effective internal communications.

Because most NTSB expenses comprise employee salaries and benefits, human capital is the most valued organizational asset. This asset requires a long-term plan to ensure its success and capabilities. The strategic objectives for Strategic Goal 4 promote the outcomes of maintaining improved human capital, encouraging teamwork, and maintaining effective communications. This strategic goal emphasizes the NTSB's challenge to devote time and resources to thinking strategically and to developing staff, while maintaining the primary commitment to investigating transportation accidents. Investing in our employees underlies our ability to maintain our investigative readiness. Our highly trained employees are skilled in identifying emerging safety issues, fully prepared to investigate accidents that may involve any of those issues and support those whose mission is the safety of the traveling public. Finally, the goal promotes strategies to ensure we foster a work environment that embraces inclusiveness, equal opportunity, and diversity.

Key Management Issues and Challenges

The NTSB has earned a reputation for thorough and independent investigation of transportation accidents. To maintain that reputation, we are committed to the continuing development of our managerial, leadership, and workforce skills comparable to the quality of the accident investigations for which we are well known. This initiative includes the entire NTSB organization—investigative offices, business support offices, and agency leadership. We are faced with the challenge of developing our workforce in an environment of technological changes and dwindling resources.

This challenge is addressed by effective long-range planning and excellent communications. Long-range planning in human capital management, as well as core operations, ensures that the NTSB is fully equipped to deal with any future investigative need. The NTSB's enhanced focus on planning results in staff and processes that are capable and flexible to deal with any and all issues and challenges. Effective communications at all levels of the organization ensure that we continually improve our plans and processes. We will devote time and resources to thinking strategically and developing our staff. To achieve our long-term vision, we must effectively plan and communicate while maintaining our primary commitment to investigating transportation accidents. We believe that initiatives currently in place will provide the necessary balance to ensure success with this strategic goal.

Strategic Objectives

1. Integrate Long-range Planning in All Elements of NTSB Business

We will make strategic planning integral elements of how the NTSB conducts business. Consistent with the requirements set out in the Government Performance Results Act of 1993 (GPRA), we will develop a comprehensive multiyear strategic plan and issue a revised plan every 3 years. In addition to these revisions, we will conduct annual reviews and updates of our strategic goals and objectives, focusing on selected performance measures each year. In addition, we will develop and update long-range plans for all aspects of our operations, including internal communications, advocacy, human capital, training, and IT, all of which are in alignment with the NTSB Strategic Plan.

2. Align and Improve Human Capital Planning

We will ensure that the quality of our management and leadership is on par with the excellence of our accident investigations. In support of this initiative, we will develop a greater focus and teamwork among both our staff and line leadership. As part of this effort, the management team will meet regularly and will set cross-office goals.

We will continue to invest in training, developing, and retaining employees, our most important and valuable asset, and will take steps to enhance our recruitment and hiring processes. We will select well-qualified applicants to fill vacancies and expand the NTSB's technical capabilities, as hiring such individuals is crucial to accomplishing our investigative mission. In addition, we will develop the skill sets of current staff through formal and informal training, as well as invest in cross-training to build individual employee skills and strengthen the NTSB's workforce. We will ensure successful achievement of these efforts through the implementation of the Strategic Human Capital Plan and the Strategic Training and Development Plan, two agency human resource plans that support human capital efforts. These two plans, which are directly aligned with the NTSB Strategic Plan, dovetail and complement each other. The Strategic Human Capital Plan includes eight key strategies to ensure that the NTSB workforce is competent, the management team is fully aligned, and that human capital strategies are implemented using a project management approach. The eight objectives are listed here:

Human Capital Strategic Objectives

- Enhance the recruitment process for critical occupations to attract well qualified applicants.
- Develop an NTSB Strategic Training Plan and ensure that workforce has access to continuing training opportunities.
- Provide for the continued recruitment and retention of a highly skilled diverse workforce.
- Raise level of awareness of supervisory and management officials regarding leadership and management as perceived by the workforce.
- Strengthen the Performance Management System to align with organizational goals and objectives.
- Outline strategies for succession planning.
- Develop an NTSB Strategic Human Capital Plan that aligns with the NTSB Strategic Plan.
- Monitor and evaluate the execution of human capital strategic objectives via a project plan.

By using the OPM Human Capital Assessment and Accountability Framework (HCAAF), the NTSB has segmented key courses of action into five critical components of human capital. These components are strategic alignment, leadership and knowledge management, results-oriented performance culture, talent management, and accountability. Implementation of our human capital plan already includes, or will include, a new performance management system, a redefinition of the job analysis process, alternative recruitment efforts, and an annual assessment of human capital management and compliance. All of this will be done to ensure the most diverse workforce available.

3. Maintain a Competent and Effective Workforce through Targeted Training and Employee Development

The investigative staff of the NTSB has a well-deserved reputation as the world's premier cadre of transportation accident investigators. However, NTSB workforce departures are one internal factor that could affect our ability to achieve organizational goals. Anticipated retirements may have a significant impact within the agency management levels during the next few years. Because the retirements will affect institutional knowledge, employee development is very important. Moreover, to function successfully, the workforce will require updated training to close the skills gap in a future environment that includes advanced management tools, and updated networking capabilities. We will ensure that staff has regular opportunities to participate in the advanced technical training and professional development essential to maintaining and advancing their critical investigative skills.

We will build our management and leadership skills for the long term, thus ensuring that we are prepared to fill the agency's leadership ranks. Our management team will ensure that all staff members have the opportunity to pursue training opportunities that will contribute to the development of their management, leadership, and job-specific skills. We will ensure that management and leadership development is an integral part of annual performance planning. The NTSB Strategic Training and Development Plan is designed to complement the agency strategic plan by focusing on specific strategies and performance measures pertaining to training. The strategies are listed below:

Strategic Training & Development Objectives:
- Ensure NTSB Training Programs are in Alignment with the Strategic Plan.
- Foster Leadership Commitment to Ensure Accomplishment of Training Objectives.
- Increase Competencies of the NTSB Workforce through Training and Development.
- Ensure the Training Curriculum Reflects Emerging Needs and the Best Strategies.
- Create an Environment of Continuous Improvement and Lifelong Learning.
- Ensure that the Evaluation of Training and Development Programs Promotes Continuous Improvement.
- Increase Available Pool of Successors for Designated Positions (Succession Management).

As the NTSB embarks on efforts to improve its strategic management of human capital, training and development will play a key role. The NTSB Strategic Training and Development Plan emphasizes leadership development and succession planning, which are critical for ensuring the agency's continued success in meeting our investigative mandate. Our succession management approach focuses on developing the talent pool at the agency through the selection of individuals for the Management Development and Executive Development programs, as well as the roll-out and implementation of the overall succession management program for the agency. Our training initiatives are designed to ensure equal opportunity.

The Training and Development Plan highlights the models and best practices relied upon by the NTSB in reviewing, strategically aligning, improving, and charting a course for its training and development program. Our approach incorporates best practices from within and outside the agency, along with a plan for continuously evaluating our progress toward strategic training and development objectives derived from the agency's Strategic Plan and Strategic Human Capital Plan. Through implementation of these plans, the NTSB will be able to use our resources wisely to ensure that our workforce possesses the necessary competencies to accomplish the agency's mission, both now and in the future.

4. Foster Effective Internal Communications

We will pursue a comprehensive strategy aimed at improving the quality of communication and cooperation, both across NTSB office boundaries and up and down the entire organization. Communication, cooperation, and teamwork will be included in management performance evaluations. Our Internal Communications Plan outlines a number of strategies and action steps to improve communication within the organization, as well as associated performance measures to gauge the level of success. The principal method we use to evaluate improved communications is the biennial (formerly annual) communications survey, which has been conducted three times thus far. The results of this survey have shown noted improvements over the 3-year period, and we expect positive communications to continue to grow at all levels of the organization.

Environmental Analysis

The NTSB's ability to achieve our strategic goals may be influenced by the changing balance of industry operations, other Federal, state, and local government activities, national priorities, market forces, and resource availability. This section discusses significant external and internal factors that could significantly impair the agency's ability to achieve our strategic goals.

External Factors

Demographic Trends

Within the next 25 years, the U.S. population is estimated to grow to 364 million, up from 282 million in 2000. Highway vehicle miles of travel are projected to increase by approximately 60 percent from 2000 to 2030, potentially leading to much higher numbers of highway crashes and fatalities. Protecting segments of the population who remain at heightened risk—including teenage and older drivers, motorcyclists, and rural residents—will require targeted safety programs. Significant increases in the older population (the number of people between the ages of 65 and 84 will increase by 114 percent from 2000 to 2050) will pose greater highway and motor vehicle safety challenges, whether older Americans are drivers or passengers.

Major Transportation Disasters

One or more catastrophic transportation accidents could severely affect the NTSB's ability to achieve our strategic goals. When catastrophic accidents occur, there is often a high level of industry, political, and public concern to determine the cause. This concern, combined with the complexity that often accompanies the investigation of transportation disasters, will require the time and attention of an undetermined number of the most skilled and experienced investigators at the agency.

New Technologies

Technological development in the transportation industry could pose a significant challenge to the achievement of our goals. Dramatic technological developments could outstrip our ability to train staff and redeploy resources. Among the developments we expect are hydrogen-fueled automobiles, increased use of composite materials, increasingly complex avionics, and increased operation of unmanned aerial vehicles, ultra-light jets, and personal-use aircraft. Our work with Emerging Issues will help address these technology challenges.

The NTSB has issued several recommendations concerning the implementation of technologies to improve highway safety. These technologies include adaptive cruise control, brake assist, anti-lock braking systems, advanced airbags, backing-up warning sensors, drowsy-driver monitoring, warning devices for specific types of impending crashes (rear-end, lane/road departure, intersection), and systems that take control of the vehicle in certain circumstances, such as electronic stability control, rollover prevention, and alcohol detection.

Additional occupant protection improvements, including advanced vehicle structures, safety belt/ignition-interlock systems, airbags and other interior protection features will reduce injuries and fatalities when crashes occur. For example, immediately after impact, using sensors, onboard communications could automatically notify rescue services of a crash, its location, and the probable extent of injuries. As these and other technologies become widely used, NTSB staff will need to be well educated about new technology to produce salient recommendations that will continue to raise the bar on safety.

Budgetary Constraints

Any major decrease in resources devoted to the NTSB and accident investigation will have a negative impact on the agency's ability to achieve our goals for this planning period. The growth in the Federal budget deficit in recent years, including the explosive increase in 2009, means that the current administration will need to address these shortfalls. Because Federal agencies, including the NTSB, must absorb personnel expenses, e.g. within-grade pay increases and annual cost-of-living adjustments, a budget increase is necessary just to maintain the salaries of the current staffing level. Therefore, a flat budget for a subsequent year implies that staff levels must decrease in order to absorb salary adjustments. If this should occur, the NTSB will be in a more difficult position to meet our investigative mandate.

Internal Factors

Staffing Shortages Due to Retirements

The average age of NTSB employees is 48.6 years, almost 2 years older than the government wide average. The NTSB workforce also includes considerably fewer employees under the age of 35, which is likely due to the need for investigative staff to possess broad industry knowledge in addition to investigative or related skills. Developing this diverse skill set usually occurs over a period of years—which is why midcareer accessions dominate among investigative and some other occupational specialties at the NTSB.

Twenty-one percent of investigators, and more than a quarter (27 percent) of the agency's senior executives, are age 60 or older; nearly 20 percent of the NTSB workforce is currently eligible to retire. Although historical trends indicate that only a portion of employees eligible to retire actually do so, the time needed to cultivate future leaders warrants serious attention to succession planning to ensure continuity of leadership. And because many of the investigative personnel occupy positions requiring unique expertise, the failure to anticipate and prepare for their eventual retirement could leave the NTSB severely hampered in our ability to accomplish our investigative mission.

Skill Gap Issues

To be successful, the NTSB relies on the outstanding skills and professionalism of our employees. As stated above, NTSB workforce departures are the one internal factor that could affect our ability to achieve organizational goals. In addition, due to budgetary reasons, anticipated retirements may have a significant impact within agency management levels during the next few years. Because these retirements will affect institutional knowledge, the training of successors is of paramount importance. Moreover, to function successfully, the aging workforce likely will require updated training to be prepared for a future environment that will include advanced management tools, new hardware and software platforms, and updated networking capabilities. Aggressive marketing, outreach, and recruitment initiatives will be necessary to attract highly skilled and diverse candidates to staff the next generation of employees and managers. We have been working to identify a number of competency and skills groups that might experience significant gaps if training and recruitment efforts are not successful. In some cases, these competency groups are already experiencing gaps. The Strategic Human Capital Plan calls for a Talent Management system that, along with strategies and action steps described in the Training and Development Plan, will address competency gaps—particularly in mission-critical occupations—by implementing and maintaining programs to attract, acquire, develop, promote, and retain quality talent.

Succession Management

The NTSB uses the Office of Personnel Management's (OPM) Strategic Leadership Management Model to assist in planning, implementing, and evaluating our succession management program. The model uses a five-step approach to the succession management process: (1) Establish strategic alignment; (2) Identify succession targets (positions) and analyze talent pool; (3) Develop Succession Management Plan; (4) Implement Succession Management Plan; and (5) Evaluate succession strategies. Even using this approach, the agency will face significant challenges in filling leadership positions in the future.

Mindful of the large number of retirement-eligible employees in the workforce and the need for highly specialized knowledge in the face of rapidly changing technology, the NTSB is committed to succession planning to avoid the potential for disruption in the effective management of the agency. A pool of candidates must be developed to ensure that, when key vacancies arise, someone with the requisite competencies is available to step in and provide continuity of leadership. Moreover, the pool must be sufficiently large to ensure the likelihood that the ideal mix of skills can be found and that the merit system principles inherent in open competition are truly practicable. In addition to building the pool through our efforts to improve training across the board, the agency has embraced the need for additional sources of diverse candidates as part of a viable succession plan that ensures equal opportunity and adheres to merit system principles.

Improper Payments Elimination and Recovery Act (IPERA) Compliance

Only a small portion of the NTSB budget is subject to IPERA reporting. The vast majority of NTSB payments are to employees in the form of payroll and travel reimbursement and intergovernmental payments such as those to Department of the Interior's National Business Center for financial services and to General Services Administration for rent. Payments subject to the Act are primarily vendor payments.

For FY2010, we made approximately 8,600 payments totaling about $19 million. For FY2011, we made approximately 14,200 payments totaling about $18 million.

NTSB is committed to minimizing the risk of improper payments. We utilize a variety of system controls, separation of duties, and other procedures to reduce that risk and to promptly identify any such payments that might occur. These controls are tested as part of the SAS70, A-123, and financial statement audit processes and are also considered during the annual FMFIA process.

Given these controls, we have estimated the improper payments rate to be less than 0.01% and the improper payments amount to be $1,800 or less. This level is below the threshold established by OMB and therefore does not represent significant improper payments. Accordingly, no plan is proposed to further reduce improper payments nor is a recovery audit program cost effective.

**U.S. Department of
Transportation**
Office of the Secretary
of Transportation

Office of Inspector General
Washington, DC 20590

November 7, 2011

The Honorable Deborah A. P. Hersman
Chairman
National Transportation Safety Board
490 L'Enfant Plaza SW
Washington, D.C. 20594

Dear Chairman Hersman:

I respectfully submit our report on the quality control review (QCR) of the National Transportation Safety Board's (NTSB) audited financial statements for fiscal years 2011 and 2010.

The audit of NTSB's financial statements as of and for the years ended September 30, 2011, and September 30, 2010, was completed by Leon Snead & Company, P.C., of Rockville, Maryland (see Enclosure), under contract to the Office of Inspector General. The contract required the audit to be performed in accordance with generally accepted Government auditing standards and Office of Management and Budget Bulletin 07-04, "Audit Requirements for Federal Financial Statements," as amended.

Leon Snead & Company, P.C. concluded that the financial statements present fairly, in all material respects, the financial position, net cost, changes in net position, and budgetary resources of NTSB, as of and for the years ended September 30, 2011, and September 30, 2010, in conformity with U.S. generally accepted accounting principles. The report did not include any reportable internal control deficiencies or instances of reportable noncompliance with laws and regulations tested.

We performed a QCR of Leon Snead & Company, P.C.'s report and related documentation. Our QCR, as differentiated from an audit performed in accordance with generally accepted Government auditing standards, was not intended for us to

Report Number QC-2012-005

express, and we do not express, an opinion on NTSB's financial statements or conclusions about the effectiveness of internal controls or compliance with laws and regulations. Leon Snead & Company, P.C. is responsible for its report dated November 4, 2011, and the conclusions expressed in that report. However, our QCR disclosed no instances in which Leon Snead & Company, P.C. did not comply, in all material respects, with generally accepted Government auditing standards. Because Leon Snead & Company, P.C. did not make any recommendations, a response to this report is not required.

We appreciate the cooperation and assistance of representatives of NTSB and Leon Snead & Company, P.C. If we can answer any questions, please call me at (202) 366-1407, or Earl C. Hedges, Program Director, at (410) 962-1729.

Sincerely,

Louis C. King
Assistant Inspector General for Financial and
Information Technology Audits

Enclosure

Report Number QC-2012-005

LEON SNEAD
& COMPANY, P.C.

Certified Public Accountants
& Management Consultants

416 Hungerford Drive, Suite 400
Rockville, Maryland 20850
301-738-8190
fax: 301-738-8210
leonsnead.companypc@erols.com

Inspector General, U.S. Department of Transportation
Chairman, National Transportation Safety Board

Independent Auditor's Report

We have audited the balance sheets of the National Transportation Safety Board (NTSB) as of September 30, 2011 and 2010, and the related statements of net cost, changes in net position, and budgetary resources (the financial statements) for the years then ended. The objective of our audit was to express an opinion on the fair presentation of those financial statements. In connection with our audit, we also considered the NTSB's internal control over financial reporting and tested the NTSB's compliance with certain provisions of applicable laws and regulations that could have a direct and material effect on its financial statements.

SUMMARY

As stated in our opinion on the financial statements, we found that the NTSB's financial statements as of and for the years ended September 30, 2011 and 2010, are presented fairly, in all material respects, in conformity with accounting principles generally accepted in the United States of America.

Our consideration of internal control would not necessarily disclose all deficiencies in internal control over financial reporting that might be material weaknesses under standards issued by the American Institute of Certified Public Accountants. However, our testing of internal control identified no material weaknesses in financial reporting.

The results of our tests of compliance with certain provisions of laws and regulations disclosed no instance of noncompliance that is required to be reported herein under *Government Auditing Standards*, issued by the Comptroller General of the United States and Office of Management and Budget (OMB) Bulletin No. 07-04, *Audit Requirements for Federal Financial Statements* (as amended).

The following sections discuss in more detail our opinion on the NTSB's financial statements, our consideration of the NTSB's internal control over financial reporting, our tests of the NTSB's compliance with certain provisions of applicable laws and regulations, and management's and our responsibilities.

OPINION ON THE FINANCIAL STATEMENTS

We have audited the accompanying balance sheets of the NTSB as of September 30, 2011 and 2010, and the related statements of net cost, changes in net position, and budgetary resources for the years then ended.

In our opinion, the financial statements referred to above present fairly, in all material respects, the financial position, net cost, changes in net position, and budgetary resource of the NTSB as of and for the years ended September 30, 2011 and 2010, in conformity with accounting principles generally accepted in the United States of America.

The information in the Management's Discussion and Analysis section is not a required part of the basic financial statements but is supplementary information required by accounting principles generally accepted in the United States of America or OMB Circular A-136, *Financial Reporting Requirements*. We have applied certain limited procedures, which consisted principally of inquiries of NTSB management regarding the methods of measurement and presentation of the supplementary information and analysis of the information for consistency with the financial statements. However, we did not audit the information and express no opinion on it. The Performance and Accountability Report, except for Management's Discussion and Analysis, is not a required part of the basic financial statements. Such information has not been subjected to the auditing procedures applied in the audit of the basic financial statements and, accordingly, we express no opinion on it.

INTERNAL CONTROL OVER FINANCIAL REPORTING

In planning and performing our audit of the financial statements of the NTSB as of and for the years ended September 30, 2011 and 2010, in accordance with auditing standards generally accepted in the Unites States of America, we considered the NTSB's internal control over financial reporting (internal control) as a basis for designing our auditing procedures for the purpose of expressing our opinion on the financial statements, but not for the purpose of expressing an opinion on the effectiveness of the NTSB's internal control. Accordingly, we do not express an opinion on the effectiveness of the NTSB's internal control.

Because of inherent limitations in internal controls, including the possibility of management override of controls, misstatements, losses, or noncompliance may nevertheless occur and not be detected. A control deficiency exists when the design or operation of a control does not allow management or employees, in the normal course of performing their assigned functions, to prevent or detect misstatements on a timely basis. A material weakness is a deficiency, or combination of deficiencies, in internal control, such that there is a reasonable possibility that a material misstatement of the financial statements will not be prevented or detected and corrected on a timely basis. A significant deficiency is a deficiency, or a combination of deficiencies, in internal control that is less severe than a material weakness, yet important enough to merit attention by those charged with governance of the NTSB.

Our consideration of internal control was for the limited purpose described in the first paragraph in this section of the report and would not necessarily identify all deficiencies in internal control that might be deficiencies, significant deficiencies or material weaknesses. We did not identify any deficiencies in internal control that we consider to be material weaknesses, as defined above.

A summary of the status of prior year findings is included as Appendix 1.

We noted another control deficiency over financial reporting that we do not consider a significant deficiency, but still needs to be addressed by management. We have reported this matter to the management of the NTSB, and those charged with governance in a separate letter dated November 4, 2011.

COMPLIANCE WITH LAWS AND REGULATIONS

The results of our tests of compliance with certain provisions of laws and regulations, as described in the Responsibilities section of this report, disclosed no instance of noncompliance with laws and regulations that is required to be reported under *Government Auditing Standards* and OMB Bulletin 07-04 (as amended), *Audit Requirements for Federal Financial Statements*.

RESPONSIBILITIES

Management Responsibilities

Management of the NTSB is responsible for: (1) preparing the financial statements in conformity with generally accepted accounting principles; (2) establishing, maintaining, and assessing internal control to provide reasonable assurance that the broad control objectives of the FMFIA are met; and (3) complying with applicable laws and regulations. In fulfilling this responsibility, estimates and judgments by management are required to assess the expected benefits and related costs of internal control policies.

Auditor Responsibilities

Our responsibility is to express an opinion on the financial statements based on our audit. We conducted our audit in accordance with auditing standards generally accepted in the United States of America; the standards applicable to financial audits contained in *Government Auditing Standards*, issued by the Comptroller General of the United States; and OMB Bulletin 07-04 (as amended). Those standards require that we plan and perform the audit to obtain reasonable assurance about whether the financial statements are free of material misstatement.

An audit includes: (1) examining, on a test basis, evidence supporting the amounts and disclosures in the financial statements; (2) assessing the accounting principles used and significant estimates made by management, as well as evaluating the overall financial statement presentation. We believe that our audit provides a reasonable basis for our opinion.

In planning and performing our audit, we considered the NTSB's internal control over financial reporting by obtaining an understanding of the agency's internal control, determining whether internal controls had been placed in operation, assessing control risk, and performing tests of controls in order to determine our auditing procedures for the purpose of expressing our opinion on the financial statements.

We limited our internal control testing to those controls necessary to achieve the objectives described in OMB Bulletin 07-04 (as amended) and *Government Auditing Standards*. We did not test all internal controls relevant to operating objectives as broadly defined by FMFIA. Our procedures were not designed to provide an opinion on internal control over financial reporting. Consequently, we do not express an opinion thereon.

As required by OMB Bulletin 07-04 (as amended), with respect to internal control related to performance measures determined to be key and reported in Management's Discussion and Analysis, we made inquiries of management concerning the methods of preparing the information, including whether it was measured and presented within prescribed guidelines; changes in the methods of measurement or presentation from those used in the prior period(s) and the reasons for any such changes; and significant assumptions or interpretations underlying the measurement or presentation. We also evaluated the consistency of Management's Discussion and Analysis with management's responses to the foregoing inquiries, audited financial statements, and other audit evidence obtained during the examination of the financial statements. Our procedures were not designed to provide assurance on internal control over reported performance measures, and, accordingly, we do not provide an opinion thereon.

AGENCY COMMENTS

The Chief Financial Officer in a memorandum dated November 4, 2011, stated that he concurred with the audit report.

DISTRIBUTION

This report is intended solely for the information and use of agency governance, management, U.S. Department of Transportation, Office of Inspector General, others within the NTSB, OMB, and Congress, and is not intended to be and should not be used by anyone other than these specified parties.

Leon Snead & Company, P.C.
November 4, 2011

Appendix 1

Status of Prior Year Reportable Conditions, and
Non-Compliance with Significant Laws and Regulations

Prior Year Condition	Status As Of September 30, 2011
Significant Deficiency: NTSB had not fully implemented a managerial cost accounting system. While the agency is able to prepare its Statement of Net Cost, and related footnote disclosures, the costs associated with these statements and disclosures are allocated to its responsibilities segments based upon estimates of "direct" salaries for various units within the agency which account for about one-half of the costs, and an allocation of remaining NTSB "common" costs.	**Substantial Improvements Made.** NTSB has designed and implemented a cost accounting system. The system was pilot tested during early 2011 and implemented agency-wide about May 2011. The agency is still compiling cost data, and will not be able to use the system to assist in the preparation of its 2011 financial statements. This issue, however, has been downgraded to a management letter deficiency.

Appendix 2

National Transportation Safety Board
Washington, D.C. 20594

Office of the Chief Financial Officer

November 4, 2011

TO: Leon Snead
          Partner

FROM: Steven E. Goldberg
          Chief Financial Officer

SUBJECT: DRAFT AUDIT REPORT
          Fiscal Year 2011 and 2010 Financial Statement Audit Report

The National Transportation Safety Board (NTSB) has reviewed the draft fiscal years 2011 and 2010 Financial Statement Audit Report and we concur with the facts and conclusions in the report. We will share the final audit report with senior officials, other interested program managers and staff.

Please convey my appreciation to everyone on your staff who worked diligently on our financial statement audit. If you have any questions or comments, please contact me or Edward Benthall at (202) 314-6241.

cc: George Banks, Program Director,
          Financial Audits, DOT OIG

Limitations of the Financial Statements

Responsibility for the integrity and objectivity of the financial information presented in the financial statements lies with NTSB management. The accompanying financial statements are prepared to report the financial policies and results of the operations of the NTSB, pursuant to the requirements of Chapter 31, of the United States Code section 3515(b). Although these statements have been prepared from the books and records of the NTSB, these financial statements are in addition to the financial reports used to monitor and control budgetary resources, which are prepared from the same books and records. The financial statements should be read with the realization that the NTSB is an agency of the Executive Branch of the United States Government, a sovereign entity. Accordingly, unfunded liabilities reported in the statements cannot be liquidated without the enactment of an appropriation, and ongoing operations are subjected to enactment of appropriations.

Management Integrity: Controls, Compliance and Challenges

The NTSB conducts an annual review of the adequacy of the agency's management accountability and controls program in accordance with the Federal Manager's Financial Integrity Act, revised OMB Circular A-123, "Management's Responsibility for Internal Control."

The results of this review are included in the Chairman's Statement of Assurance sent to the President on September 30, 2011. The Chairman's assurance is based on NTSB Office Director Management Control Assurance Memorandums and NTSB responses to Office Directors, Division Chiefs, and other Program Managers Risk Assessments for An Accountability Unit conducted in accordance with the OMB's guidance in Circular A-123, "Management's Responsibility for Internal Control."

The NTSB also relies on the findings and results of audits and studies conducted by the Department of Transportation, Office of Inspector General (DOT-OIG), Government Accountability Office, other audits and reviews, and the results of our financial statement audit, conducted under the Chief Financial Officers Act of 1990, the Accountability of Tax Dollars Act of 2002, and OMB Circular A-136.

As of September 30, 2011, there is no new material weakness to report.

Discussion and Analysis of Financial Statements

The NTSB's FY 2011 and 2010 financial statements report the agency's financial position and results of operations on an accrual basis. These annual financial statements comprise a Balance Sheet, Statement of Net Cost, Statement of Changes in Net Position, Statement of Budgetary Resources, and related notes that provide a clear description of the agency and its mission, as well as the significant accounting policies used to develop the statements.

Consolidated Balance Sheet

The major components of the Consolidated Balance Sheet are assets, liabilities, and net position.

ASSETS. Assets represent agency resources that have future economic benefits.

The NTSB's assets totaled $54.3 million in FY 2011. Fund balances with the U.S. Treasury—mostly undisbursed cash balances from appropriated funds—comprised about 72 percent of the total assets. The NTSB does not maintain any cash balances outside of the U.S. Treasury and does not have any revolving or trust funds. Less than 1 percent of the NTSB's assets were composed of accounts receivable, which reflects funds owed to the NTSB by other Federal agencies and the public. The value of equipment, less accumulated depreciation, was $15.4 million.

LIABILITIES. Liabilities are recognized when they are incurred, regardless of whether they are carried by budgetary resources. In FY 2011, the NTSB had total liabilities of $33.6 million. The largest components of these liabilities were a capital lease liability of $16.9 million. Accounts payable reflect funds owed primarily for contracts and other services.

NET POSITION. The NTSB's net position, which reflects the difference between assets and liabilities and represents the agency's financial condition, totals $20.7 million. This amount is broken into two categories: unexpended appropriations (amounts related to undelivered orders and unobligated balances) of $29.4 million and cumulative results of operations (net results of operations since inception plus purchases of capital assets) of negative $8.7 million. Cumulative result of operations reflects a deficit due to the recording of unfunded items such as annual leave and workers compensation liabilities.

Consolidated Statement of Net Cost

The Consolidated Statement of Net Cost represents the net cost to operate the agency. Net costs are composed of gross costs less earned revenues and are reported by the NTSB's major programs. The NTSB's FY 2011 net cost of operations was $96.4 million: $98.8 million in gross costs less $2.4 million in earned revenues.

Consolidated Statement of Changes in Net Position

The Consolidated Statement of Changes in Net Position reports the changes in net position during the reporting period. The NTSB ended FY 2011 with a net position total of $20.7 million, a positive change in net position.

Combined Statement of Budgetary Resources

The Combined Statement of Budgetary Resources focuses on how budgetary resources (appropriations and offsetting collections) were made available, the status of those resources (obligated or unobligated) at the end of the reporting period, and the relationship between budgetary resources and outlays (collections and disbursements). The NTSB's FY 2011 budgetary resources totaled $120.2 million and primarily consisted of budget authority funds of $97.8 million and unobligated balance of $20.5 million.

Accrual Basis of Accounting

Method of accounting that recognizes revenue when earned rather than when collected and recognizes expenses when incurred rather than when paid.

When: The order is placed.
Then: The obligation is recorded as an undelivered order.

When: The materials are received and accepted.
Then: The obligational authority is expended and an accounts payable is recorded.

When: The payment is made.
Then: An outlay occurs and the account payable is cleared.

NATIONAL TRANSPORTATION SAFETY BOARD
Balance Sheet
As of September 30, 2011 and 2010

Assets		FY 2011		FY 2010
Intragovernmental:				
Fund balance with Treasury (Note 2)	$	38,861,943	$	38,566,572
Total Intragovernmental Assets	$	38,861,943	$	38,566,572
Accounts receivable (Note 3)	$	4,366	$	6,464
Property and equipment, net (Note 4)		15,425,571		16,275,905
	$	15,429,937	$	16,282,369
Total Assets	**$**	**54,291,880**	**$**	**54,848,941**
Liabilities				
Intragovernmental:				
Accounts payable (Note 7)	$	149,202	$	-
Other liabilities (Note 7)		1,363,332		1,425,640
Total Intragovernmental	$	1,512,534	$	1,425,640
Accounts payable (Note 7)	$	2,222,021	$	3,923,426
Federal Employee Benefits (Note 7)		6,743,644		6,831,005
Capital lease liability (Note 8)		16,937,062		17,936,665
Other Liabilities (Note 7)		6,138,326		7,933,763
Total Liabilities	**$**	**33,553,587**	**$**	**38,050,499**
Net Position				
Unexpended appropriations	$	29,354,347	$	25,889,307
Cumulative results of operations		(8,616,054)		(9,090,865)
Total Net Position	**$**	**20,738,293**	**$**	**16,798,442**
Total Liabilities and Net Position	**$**	**54,291,880**	**$**	**54,848,941**

The accompanying notes are an integral part of these statements.

NATIONAL TRANSPORTATION SAFETY BOARD
Statement of Net Cost
For the Years Ending September 30, 2011 and 2010

	FY 2011	FY 2010
	Aviation Safety	**Aviation Safety**
Gross costs	$ 50,580,075	$ 49,121,810
Less: Earned Revenue	(1,333,074)	(1,827,204)
Net Costs (Note 9)	$ 49,247,001	$ 47,294,606
	Surface Transportation Safety	**Surface Transportation Safety**
Gross costs	$ 29,691,860	$ 29,515,580
Less: Earned Revenue	(663,138)	(1,072,011)
Net Costs (Note 9)	$ 29,028,722	$ 28,443,569
	Research & Engineering	**Research & Engineering**
Gross costs	$ 18,570,778	$ 17,268,723
Less: Earned Revenue	(405,674)	(598,728)
Net Costs (Note 9)	$ 18,165,104	$ 16,669,995
Net Cost of Operations	$ **96,440,827**	$ **92,408,170**

The accompanying notes are an integral part of these statements.

NATIONAL TRANSPORTATION SAFETY BOARD
Consolidated Statement of Changes in Net Position
For the Years Ending September 30, 2011 and 2010

	FY 2011 Cumulative Results of Operations	FY 2010 Cumulative Results of Operations
Beginning Balances	($9,090,865)	($10,286,289)
Prior period adjustments (+/-)	-	-
Beginning balances, as adjusted	($9,090,865)	($10,286,289)
Budgetary Financing Sources:		
Appropriations used	$93,208,249	$89,731,880
Other Financing Sources:		
Imputed financing from costs absorbed by others	3,707,389	3,871,714
Total Financing Sources	$96,915,638	$93,603,594
Net Cost of Operations (+/-)	($96,440,827)	($92,408,170)
Net Change	$474,811	$1,195,424
Cumulative Results of Operations	**($8,616,054)**	**($9,090,865)**

	FY 2011 Unexpended Appropriations	FY 2010 Unexpended Appropriations
Beginning Balances	$25,889,307	$18,649,872
Prior period adjustments (+/-)	-	-
Beginning balances, as adjusted	$25,889,307	$18,649,872
Budgetary Financing Sources:		
Appropriations received	$97,853,900	$98,050,000
Other adjustments (rescissions, etc) (+/-)	(1,180,611)	(1,078,685)
Appropriations used	(93,208,249)	(89,731,880)
Total Budgetary Financing Sources	$3,465,040	$7,239,435
Total Unexpended Appropriations	**$29,354,347**	**$25,889,307**
Net Position	**$20,738,293**	**$16,798,442**

The accompanying notes are an integral part of these statements.

NATIONAL TRANSPORTATION SAFETY BOARD
Statement of Budgetary Resources
For the Years Ending September 30, 2011 and 2010

Budgetary Resources:		FY 2011		FY 2010
Unobligated balance:				
Unobligated Balance, Brought Forward, October 1	$	18,476,412	$	11,377,159
		-		
Recoveries of prior year obligations: actual		2,548,137		1,547,206
Budget authority:				
Appropriation		97,853,900		98,050,000
Spending from Offsetting Collections				
Earned				
Collected		2,524,076		3,473,123
Change in Receivables from Federal sources				
Change in Unfilled Orders				
Advance Received				
Without Advance from Federal sources				
Anticipated for rest of year, without advances		-		-
Permanently not available		(1,180,611)		(1,078,685)
Total Budgetary Resources (Note 10)	$	**120,221,914**		**113,368,803**
Status of Budgetary Resources:				
Obligations Incurred:				
Direct				
Category A (Note 10)	$	97,842,472		92,832,346
Reimbursable: Category B (Note 10)		1,836,887		2,060,045
	$	99,679,359		94,892,391
Unobligated Balance				
Apportioned Balance Currently Available	$	8,906,028		10,906,618
Anticipated		-		-
Unobligated balance not available		11,636,527		7,569,794
Total Unobligated Balances	$	20,542,555		18,476,412
Total Status of Budgetary Resources	$	**120,221,914**		**113,368,803**
Change in Obligated Balance:				
Obligated Balance, net:				
Unpaid Obligations, Brought Forward, October 1	$	20,090,160		15,880,053
Uncollected customer payments from Federal sources, brought forward, October 1				
Obligations Incurred		99,679,359		94,892,391
Less: Gross Outlays		(98,901,994)	$	(89,135,078)
Obligated Balance transfers, net				
Less: Recoveries of prior year unpaid obligations, actual		(2,548,137)		(1,547,206)
Change in uncollected customer payments from Federal sources				
Obligated Balance, net, end of period:				
Unpaid obligations	$	18,319,388		20,090,160
Uncollected customer payments from Federal sources		-		-
Total, unpaid obligated balance, net, end of period	$	18,319,388	$	20,090,160
Net Outlays:				
Gross Outlays	$	98,901,994		89,135,078
Less: Offsetting Collections		(2,524,077)		(3,473,123)
Net Outlays (Note 10):	$	**96,377,917**	$	**85,661,955**

The accompanying notes are an integral part of these statements.

Note 1

SUMMARY OF SIGNIFICANT ACCOUNTING POLICIES

Reporting Entity

The accompanying financial statements present the financial position, net cost of operations, changes in net position and budgetary resources of the National Transportation Safety Board (NTSB). The NTSB is an independent agency charged with determining the probable cause(s) of transportation accidents and promoting transportation safety. The financial activity presented relates primarily to the execution of the NTSB's congressionally approved budget. The NTSB began operations in 1967 and, although independent, it relied on the U.S. Department of Transportation (DOT) for funding and administrative support. In 1975, under the Independent Safety Board Act, all organizational ties to DOT were severed. The NTSB is not part of DOT, or affiliated with any of its modal agencies. The laws specific to the Board are located in Chapter VIII, Title 49 of the Code of Federal Regulations.

Basis of Accounting and Presentation

These financial statements reflect both accrual and budgetary accounting transactions. Under the accrual method of accounting, revenues are recognized when earned and expenses are recognized as incurred, without regard to receipt or payment of cash. Budgetary accounting is designed to recognize the obligation of funds according to legal requirements. Budgetary accounting is essential for compliance with legal constraints and controls over the use of Federal funds.

These financial statements have been prepared from the books and reports of NTSB in accordance with U.S. generally accepted accounting principles (GAAP) for the Federal government and the Office of Management and Budget (OMB) Circular A-136.

Assets

Intragovernmental assets are those assets that arise from transactions with other Federal entities. Entity assets are available for use by the entity in its operations while nonentity assets are assets held by the entity but not available for use by the entity in its operations.

Fund Balance with U.S. Treasury

The NTSB does not maintain cash in commercial bank accounts. The U.S. Treasury processes cash receipts and disbursements. Funds with the U.S. Treasury consist of appropriated and deposited funds that are available to pay current liabilities and finance authorized purchase commitments.

Accounts Receivable

NTSB's accounts receivable represent amounts due from overpayments to current and non-current employees and from vendors. NTSB maintains an allowance for doubtful accounts for public receivables based on past collection experience. The allowance for doubtful accounts is reviewed and adjusted quarterly.

Property and Equipment

General Property and Equipment

The Office of the Chief Financial Officer has established a capitalization policy for general property and equipment (P&E). General P&E is reported at acquisition cost. The capitalization threshold is established at $25,000. General P&E consists of items that are used by NTSB to support its mission. Depreciation on these assets is calculated using the straight-line method.

The land and buildings in which the NTSB operates are primarily leased from commercial entities. The General Services Administration (GSA) provides some of the facilities occupied by the NTSB. GSA charges the NTSB a Standard Level Users Charge (SLUC) that approximates the commercial rental rates for similar properties.

Leasehold Improvements

The NTSB capitalization policy for leasehold improvements has established a capitalization threshold of $100,000. A leasehold improvement is an improvement of a leased asset that increases the asset's value. Depreciation on these assets is calculated using the straight-line method with ten years as the estimated useful life of the improvements or the remaining term of the lease, whichever is less.

Capital Lease Assets

Any Lease-to-Ownership Plans (LTOP) leases are classified as capital leases. The NTSB has one capital lease, for space rental on the building that houses the NTSB Ashburn facility. This is a twenty-year lease. Depreciation on the capital lease is calculated using the straight-line method with twenty years, the term of the lease, as the estimated useful life of the capital lease.

Internal Use Software

The capitalization threshold of internal use software is established at $250,000. Only the costs associated with the software development phase including labor are subject to capitalization. Software development phase activities generally include the design of chosen path, including software configuration and software interfaces, coding, installation to hardware and testing, including the parallel processing phase. Internal use software includes software to operate NTSB programs and software used to produce NTSB goods and services. Depreciation on these assets is calculated using the straight-line method with three years as the estimated useful life of the asset.

Liabilities

Liabilities represent amounts that are likely to be paid by the NTSB as the result of transactions or events that have already occurred; however, no liabilities are paid by the NTSB without an appropriation. Intragovernmental liabilities arise from transactions with other Federal entities.

Accounts payable

Accounts payable consist of amounts owed for goods, services and other expenses received but not yet paid.

Accrued Payroll and Benefits

Accrued Payroll and Benefits represents salaries, wages and benefits earned by employees, but not disbursed as of September 30, 2011. Accrued payroll and benefits are payable to employees and are therefore not classified as intragovernmental.

Annual, Sick, and Other Leave

Annual leave is recognized as an expense and as a liability as it is earned; the liability is reduced as leave is taken. Each year, the balance in the accrued annual, restored, and compensatory leave account is adjusted to reflect current leave balances and pay rates. Sick leave and other types of non-vested leave are expensed as taken.

Employee Retirement Plans

Civil Service Retirement System (CSRS) and Federal Employees Retirement System (FERS)

NTSB employees participate in one of two retirement programs, either the CSRS or the FERS, which became effective on January 1, 1987. Most NTSB employees hired after December 31, 1983, are automatically covered by FERS and Social Security.

For CSRS covered employees, the NTSB withheld 7.0% of gross earnings. The NTSB matches the withholding, and the sum of the withholding and the matching funds is transferred to the Civil Service Retirement System.

For each fiscal year the Office of Personnel Management (OPM) calculates the U.S. Government's service costs for covered employees, which is an estimate of the amount of funds that, if accumulated annually and invested over an employee's career, would be enough to pay that employee's future benefits. Since the U.S. Government's estimated FY 2011 service cost exceeds contributions made by employer agencies and covered employees, the plan is not fully funded by the NTSB and its employees. As of September 30, 2011, NTSB recognized $3.7 million as an imputed cost and as an imputed financing source for the difference between the estimated service cost and the contributions made by NTSB and its employees.

FERS contributions made by employer agencies and covered employees exceed the U.S. Government's estimated FY 2011 service cost. For FERS covered employees the NTSB made contributions of 11.7% of basic pay. Employees contributed .80% of gross earnings. Employees participating in FERS are covered under the Federal Insurance Contribution Act (FICA) for which the NTSB contributes a matching amount to the Social Security Administration.

Thrift Savings Plan (TSP)

Employees covered by CSRS and FERS are eligible to contribute to the U.S. Government's TSP, administered by the Federal Retirement Thrift Investment Board. The NTSB makes a mandatory contribution of 1% of basic pay for FERS-covered employees. In addition, NTSB makes matching contributions, of up to 5% of basic pay, for employees who contribute to the Thrift Savings Plan. Contributions are matched dollar for dollar for the first 3 percent of pay contributed each pay period and 50 cents on the dollar for the next 2 percent of pay. There are no percentage limits on contributions for FERS participants. There are no percentage limits for CSRS participants, but there is no governmental matching contribution. The maximum amounts that either FERS or CSRS employees may contribute to the plan in calendar year 2011 is $16,500.

The NTSB financial statements do not report CSRS or FERS assets, accumulated plan benefits, or unfunded liabilities, if any, which may be applicable to NTSB employees and funded by NTSB. Such reporting is the responsibility of OPM.

Contingencies

A contingency is an existing condition, situation, or set of circumstances involving uncertainty as to possible gain or loss. The uncertainty will ultimately be resolved when one or more future events occur or fail to occur. A contingent liability is recognized when a past event or exchange transaction has occurred, and a future outflow or other sacrifice of resources is measurable and probable. A contingency is not disclosed in the Notes to the Financial Statements when any of the conditions for liability recognition are not met and the chance of the future confirming event or events occurring is more than remote but less than probable.

The NTSB is not a party to any legal actions that are likely to result in a material liability. Accordingly, no provision for loss is included in the financial statements.

Revenues and Other Financing Sources

Appropriations

Most of NTSB's operating funds are provided by congressional appropriations of budget authority. The NTSB receives appropriations on annual, multi-year, and no-year bases. NTSB receives financial resources from the following appropriations:

Annual Salaries and Expenses Appropriation

Annual one-year appropriations are provided by Congress and are available for obligation in the fiscal year for which it was provided to fund the overall operation of the NTSB.

Supplemental Salaries and Expenses Appropriation

Supplemental appropriations provided by Congress to fund extraordinary investigations.

Two Year Appropriation for Lease Renewal Expenses

For FY 2010, Congress appropriated $2,416,000 to fund one-time expenses associated with renewing the lease for NTSB's Washington, DC headquarters. The funding was available for obligation in FY2010 and FY2011.

Two Year Appropriation

For FY2011 Congress appropriated $2.4 million. The funding is available for obligation in FY2011 and FY2012.

No Year Emergency Fund Appropriation

A no-year Emergency Fund appropriation was provided by the Congress to fund extraordinary accident investigation costs. Emergency Fund disbursements are made at the discretion of the NTSB, but must be reported to the Congress. A no-year appropriation is available for obligation without fiscal year limitation. The NTSB's Emergency Fund currently is appropriated at $1,997,884.

Imputed Financing Sources

In accordance with OMB Bulletin No. A-136, all expenses should be reported by agencies whether or not these expenses would be paid by the agency that incurs the expense. The amounts for certain expenses of the NTSB, which will be paid by other Federal agencies, are recorded in the "Statement of Net Cost." A corresponding amount is recognized in the "Statement of Changes in Net Position" as an "Imputed Financing Source." These imputed financing sources primarily represent unfunded pension costs of NTSB employees.

Statement of Net Cost

Sub-Organization Program Costs

The NTSB Statement of Net Cost is presented by Responsibility Segment. These Responsibility Segments are based on the NTSB's mission and funding sources. The major programs that comprise the Responsibility Segments are: Aviation Safety, Surface Transportation Safety, and Research and Engineering.

Earned Revenue

Earned revenues collected by NTSB include amounts collected for training programs, rental of conference room space, subleasing of office space, and for investigative related services.

Net Position

Net position is the residual difference between assets and liabilities and comprises Unexpended Appropriations and Cumulative Results of Operations.

Unexpended appropriations include appropriations not yet obligated or expended, represented by the unobligated balances and undelivered orders of NTSB's appropriated funds. Multi-year appropriations remain available to NTSB for obligation in future periods. Unobligated balances associated with appropriations that expire at the end of the fiscal year remain available for obligation adjustments, but not for new obligations, until that account is closed, five years after the appropriations expire. Cumulative Results of Operations is the Net Result of NTSB's operations since inception.

Use of Estimates

The preparation of financial statements in accordance with the accounting principles described above requires management to make estimates and assumptions that affect the amounts reported in the financial statements and accompanying footnotes. Actual results could differ from those estimates.

Note 2

FUND BALANCES WITH THE U.S. TREASURY

U.S. Treasury processes NTSB cash receipts and disbursements. Non Federal receipts are deposited in commercial banks, which transfer the receipts to the U.S. Treasury Funds with the U S Treasury represent appropriated funds and funds received in exchange for providing services. These funds are available to finance expenditures.

Fund Balance with the U S Treasury

Funds	Entity FY 2011	Non-Entity FY 2011	Total FY 2011	Entity FY 2010	Non-Entity FY 2010	Total FY 2010
Intragovernmental: Appropriated Funds	$ 38,861,943	$ -	$ 38,861,943	$ 38,566,572	$ -	$ 38,566,572
Less: Unavailable Receipts	-	-	-	-	-	-
Total	$ 38,861,943	$ -	$ 38,861,943	$ 38,566,572	$ -	$ 38,566,572

Status of Fund Balance with Treasury	FY 2011	FY 2010
Unobligated Balance		
Available	$8,906,028	$10,906,618
Unavailable	11,636,527	7,569,794
Obligated Balance Not Yet Disbursed	18,319,388	20,090,160
Total	$38,861,943	$38,566,572

Note 3

ACCOUNTS RECEIVABLE

NTSB's accounts receivable represent amounts due from overpayments to current and non-current employees and from vendors. NTSB maintains an allowance for doubtful accounts for public receivables based on past collection experience. NTSB estimates the allowance for doubtful accounts based on the following agency schedule.

Days Outstanding	Percentage
0-120	0%
Over 120 Days	100%

The allowance for doubtful accounts is reviewed and adjusted quarterly

	Interagency FY 2011	Public FY 2011	Total FY 2011	Interagency FY 2010	Public FY 2010	Total FY 2010
Gross Receivables	$ -	$ 99,027	$ 99,027	$ -	$ 103,565	$ 103,565
Allowance for Loss	$ -	$ 94,661	$ 94,661	$ -	$ 97,101	$ 97,101
Net Receivables	$ -	$ 4,366	$ 4,366	$ -	$ 6,464	$ 6,464

Note 4

PROPERTY AND EQUIPMENT, NET

Property and equipment consisted of the following as of September 30, 2011 and 2010:

Property and Equipment

Classes of Fixed Assets	Service Life (Years)	Acquisition Value FY 2011	Accumulated Depreciation FY 2011	Net Book Value FY 2011	Acquisition Value FY 2010	Accumulated Depreciation FY 2010	Net Book Value FY 2010
Desktop and laptop computers and peripherals	3	$ 544,220	$ 281,891	$ 262,329	$ 544,220	$ 100,650	$ 443,570
Other ADP and Tele-comm equipment (servers, routers)	5	$ 480,073	$ 332,867	$ 147,206	$ 419,255	$ 270,862	$ 148,393
Furniture	5	$ 731,128	$ 731,128	$ -	$ 731,128	$ 731,128	$ -
Investigative equipment	5	$ 1,266,502	$ 420,913	$ 845,589	$ 461,595	$ 235,557	$ 226,038
Office Equipment	5	$ -	$ -	$ -	$ -	$ -	$ -
Internal Use Software	3	$ 2,178,105	$ 2,149,355	$ 28,750	$ 2,178,105	$ 2,047,689	$ 130,416
Leasehold Improvements	10	$ 628,163	$ 628,163	$ -	$ 628,163	$ 628,163	$ -
Capital lease	20	$ 23,731,941	$ 9,590,244	$ 14,141,697	$ 23,731,941	$ 8,404,453	$15,327,488
Totals		$ 29,560,132	$ 14,134,561	$ 15,425,571	$ 28,694,407	$ 12,418,502	$16,275,905

Note 5

ACCRUED FECA LIABILITY

The Federal Employees' Compensation Act (FECA) provides income and medical cost protection to covered Federal civilian employees injured on the job, employees who have incurred a work-related occupational disease, and beneficiaries of employees whose death is attributable to a job-related injury or occupational disease. Claims incurred for benefits for NTSB employees under FECA are administered by the Department of Labor (DOL) and are ultimately paid by the NTSB.

FECA liability includes two components: (1) the accrued liability which represents money owed for claims paid by the DOL through the current fiscal year, for which billing to and payment by the NTSB will occur in a subsequent fiscal year, and (2) the liability for future costs which represents the expected liability for approved compensation cases beyond the current fiscal year. Estimated future costs have been actuarially determined, and are regarded as a liability to the public because neither the costs nor reimbursement have been recognized by DOL. FECA liability is included in Liabilities Not Covered by Budgetary Resources, as described in Note 7.

The NTSB accrues liabilities based on estimates of funds owed to other Federal government entities for services provided, but not yet billed. The accruals for Workers Compensation and Unemployment Compensation represent the estimated liability for the current fiscal year; for money owed, but not billed; and for claims, which were paid by the Department of Labor, but not yet billed to the NTSB.

Note 6

ACCRUED ANNUAL LEAVE

Accrued annual leave consists of employees' unpaid leave balances at September 30, 2011 and reflects wage rates in effect at quarter end. Accrued annual leave is included in Liabilities Not Covered by Budgetary Resources, as covered in Note 7.

Note 7

LIABILITIES COVERED AND NOT COVERED BY BUDGETARY RESOURCES

Liabilities Not Covered by Budgetary Resources result from the receipt of goods and services, or the occurrence of events for which appropriations, revenues, or other financing sources necessary to pay the liabilities have not yet been made available through Congressional appropriation. These include FECA and annual leave liability Liabilities Covered by Budgetary Resources are those for which budgetary resources are available in the current fiscal year. NTSB's liabilities covered and not covered by budgetary resources are as follows:

Liabilities Covered and Not Covered by Budgetary Resources

Liabilities Covered by Budgetary Resources	FY 2011	FY 2010
Employer Contribution and Payroll Taxes Payable	$244,460	$615,739
Accounts Payable	2,371,223	3,923,426
Accrued Payroll	971,467	2,557,237
	$3,587,150	$7,096,402
Liabilities Not Covered by Budgetary Resources		
Capital Lease Liability	16,937,062	17,936,665
Accrued Unfunded Annual Leave	4,922,399	4,760,787
Actuarial FECA Liability	6,743,644	6,831,005
Accrued Unfunded FECA Liability	1,363,332	1,425,640
Total Liabilities Covered and Not Covered by Budgetary Resources	**$33,553,587**	**$38,050,499**

Liabilities Covered and Not Covered by Budgetary Resources
Intragovernmental and Governmental

Intragovernmental	FY 2011	FY 2010
Accounts Payable	$ 149,202	$ -
Other Liabilities	1,363,332	1,425,640
Total Intragovernmental	**$ 1,512,534**	**$ 1,425,640**
Accounts Payable	$ 2,222,021	$ 3,923,426
Accrued Payroll	971,467	2,557,237
Employer Contribution and Payroll Taxes Payable	244,460	615,739
Capital Lease Liability	16,937,062	17,936,665
Accrued Unfunded Annual Leave	4,922,399	4,760,787
Actuarial FECA Liability	6,743,644	6,831,005
Total Liabilities Covered and Not Covered by Budgetary Resources	**$ 33,553,587**	**$ 38,050,499**

Note 8

LEASES

The NTSB has commitments under cancelable leases for office space. These leases have terms that extend up to 10 years. The majority of buildings in which the NTSB operates are leased from commercial companies. Under their lease agreement with the General Services Administration (GSA), the NTSB is charged rent that is intended to approximate commercial rental rates.

The NTSB has a 20-year capital lease for the Ashburn facility space which was entered into in 2001. The total future payments disclosed for the Ashburn facility include estimates for services and utilities.

Future Capital Lease Payments

Fiscal Year	Space Rental FY 2011	Space Rental FY 2010
2011	$ -	$2,521,440
2012	2,521,440	2,521,440
2013	2,521,440	2,521,440
2014	2,521,440	2,521,440
2015	2,521,440	2,521,440
2016	2,521,440	2,521,440
2017 and beyond	17,229,840	17,229,840
Total Future Lease Payments	**$29,837,040**	**$32,358,480**
Less: Imputed Interest	(5,965,833)	(6,901,170)
Less: Executory Costs (Maintenance)	(6,934,145)	(7,520,645)
Net Capital Lease Liability	**$16,937,062**	**$17,936,665**

In 2003 NTSB determined that this lease should be recorded as a capital lease. Capitalizing the full net present value of the Ashburn facility lease created a deficiency in 2001 funds. This deficiency was reported to OMB and Congress. OMB has provided guidance on future funding and reporting of this liability With the cancellation of the FY 2001 appropriation at September 30, 2006, the budgetary accounts no longer reflect a deficiency situation. The related asset, liability, and amortization will remain on the general ledger until the lease is fully liquidated. Annual Appropriation acts now include language to provide funds to make lease payments due in the current fiscal year.

The lease liability not covered by budgetary resources at September 30, 2011 is $16,937,062.

The NTSB has operating leases for copiers, postage meters and vehicles. Copiers and postage meters are leased on an annual basis. These leases are cancelable or renewable on an annual basis at the option of NTSB. They do not impose binding commitments on NTSB for future rental payments on leases with terms longer than one year.

Future operating payments due are as follows:

Future Operating Lease Payments at September 30, 2011

Fiscal Year	Space Rental-Headquarters and Regional Offices FY 2011	Space Rental-Headquarters and Regional Offices FY 2010
2011	$ -	6,426,578
2012	8,895,327	8,040,139
2013	8,794,920	8,067,182
2014	8,709,162	8,023,231
2015	8,600,249	7,920,927
2016	8,646,488	7,996,099
2017 and beyond	37,024,598	34,250,929
Total Future Lease payments	**$ 80,670,744**	**$ 80,725,085**

NTSB signed a new ten year lease in August 2010.

GSA vehicle leases are cancelable at any time without penalty and are not included in Future Operating Lease Payments information.

Future Lease Receipts

In August 2007, NTSB signed two sub-lease agreements to provide certain office space beginning in September 2007.

The first is with the Federal Aviation Administration (FAA) for the period of twelve months with the possibility of extension. This agreement resulted in the receipt of $451,093 over the twelve month lease term, received quarterly. The Sub-Lessee rental rate was annually adjusted by a reconciliation of Operating costs and taxes corresponding with increases to the Consumer Price Index (CPI) Cost of Living index. The agreement commenced on September 1, 2007 and expired on November 30, 2010. It was not renewed.

The second is with the Transportation Security Administration (TSA) for a period of ten years beginning October 1, 2008. The Sub-Lessee may cancel this agreement after the first twelve months with 120 days notice without penalty. This agreement will result in the receipt of $564,015 over the twelve-month lease term in accordance with amendment #3, paid quarterly. The Sub-Lessee rental rate will be annually adjusted by a reconciliation of Operating costs and taxes corresponding with increases to the Consumer Price Index (CPI) Cost of Living index.

In June 2008, NTSB signed a sub-lease agreement with the Department of Homeland Security (DHS) to provide certain office space beginning June 16, 2008.

This sub-lease was for the initial period of June 16, 2008 to September 30 2008 with four option years, paid quarterly in advance. This agreement resulted in the receipt of $327,200 over the twelve-month lease erm The Sub-Lessee rental rate will b annually adjusted by a r concili tion of Operating costs and taxes corresponding with increases to the Consumer Price Index (CPI) Cost of Living index.

Future Lease Receipts at September 30, 2011

Fisc l Year	FAA	TS	HS
20 2	$ -	56 ,0 5	$ 327,200
20 3	-	56 ,0 5	-
20 4	-	56 ,0 5	-
20 5	-	56 ,0 5	-
20 6	-	56 ,0 5	-
20 7 and eyond	-	56 ,0 5	-
T t l Futur Le se Receipts	$ -	3,3 4,090	S 327,2

Future Lease Receipts at September 30, 2010

Fiscal Year	FAA	TSA	DHS
2011	$ 27,342	$ 623,653	$ 327,200
2012	-	623,653	327,200
2013	-	623,653	-
2014	-	623,653	-
2015	-	623,653	-
2016 and beyond	-	1,247,306	-
Total Future Lease Receipts	$ 27,342	S 4,365,571	S 654,400

Note 9

STATEMENT OF NET COST

Intragovernmental and Public Costs

Fiscal Year 2011	Aviation Safety	Surface Safety	Research & Engineering	Consolidated Totals
Intragovernmental Gross Costs	$ 12,036,882	$ 7,292,962	$ 4,337,932	$ 23,667,776
Less: Intragovernmental Earned Revenue	(927,337)	(386,593)	(229,950)	(1,543,880)
Intragovernmental Net Costs	$ 11,109,545	$6,906,369	$4,107,982	$22,123,896
Gross Costs with the Public	$ 38,543,193	$ 22,398,898	$ 14,232,845	$ 75,174,936
Less: Earned Revenues from the Public	(405,737)	(276,545)	(175,723)	(858,005)
Net Costs with the Public	$ 38,137,456	$ 22,122,353	$ 14,057,122	$ 74,316,931
Net Cost of Operations	$ 49,247,001	$29,028,722	$ 18,165,104	$ 96,440,827

Fiscal Year 2010	Aviation Safety	Surface Safety	Research & Engineering	Consolidated Totals
Intragovernmental Gross Costs	$ 8,992,188	$ 5,537,346	$ 3,004,437	$ 17,533,971
Less: Intragovernmental Earned Revenue	(1,210,659)	(745,518)	(404,501)	(2,360,678)
Intragovernmental Net Costs	$ 7,781,529	$4,791,828	$2,599,936	$15,173,293
Gross Costs with the Public	$ 40,129,622	$ 23,978,234	$ 14,264,286	$ 78,372,142
Less: Earned Revenues from the Public	(616,545)	(326,493)	(194,227)	(1,137,265)
Net Costs with the Public	$ 39,513,077	$ 23,651,741	$ 14,070,059	$ 77,234,877
Net Cost of Operations	$ 47,294,606	$28,443,569	$ 16,669,995	$ 92,408,170

Note 10

STATEMENT OF BUDGETARY RESOURCES

The Statement of Budgetary Resources compares budgetary resources with the status of those resources. For September 30, 2011, and September 30, 2010, respectively, budgetary resources were $120 million and $113 million; net outlays for the year were $96 million and $86 million; direct obligations incurred against amounts apportioned under Category A were $98 million and $93 million; and the amount of direct obligations incurred against amounts apportioned under Category B were $2 million and $2 million.

	FY 2011	**FY 2010**
Budgetary Resources	$120,221,914	$113,368,803
Net Outlays	96,337,917	85,661,955
Category A Apportionments	97,842,472	92,832,346
Reimbursable Category B	1,836,887	2,060,045

The total of undelivered orders at September 30, 2011 and 2010 were $14.7 million and $13.0 million.

Note 11

EXPLANATION OF DIFFERENCES BETWEEN THE STATEMENT OF BUDGETARY RESOURCES AND THE BUDGET OF THE UNITED STATES GOVERNMENT

FY 2010 Dollars in millions	Budgetary Resources	Obligations Incurred	Offsetting Receipts	Net Outlays
Statement of Budgetary Resources	$113	$95	$-	$86
Unobligated Balance Brought Forward	$(15)	-	-	-
Budget of the U.S. Government	$98	$95	-	$86
Differences	$-	$-	$-	$-

Source: Appendix, United States Budget

FY 2010 is the latest year for which actual figures are available   The President's Budget with actual figures for FY 2011 has not yet been published. Actual figures for FY 2011 are expected to be available in January 2012 and are expected to be found at http://www.whitehouse.gov/omb/.

Note 12

NET COST OF OPERATIONS VS. BUDGET

	FY 2011	FY 2010
Resources Used to Finance Activities		
Obligations Incurred	$99,679,359	$94,892,391
Less: spending authority from offsetting collections and recoveries	(5,072,214)	(5,020,329)
Net obligations	94,607,145	89,872,062
Imputed financing from costs absorbed by others	3,707,389	3,871,714
Total resources used to finance activities	**$98,314,534**	**$93,743,776**
Resources Used to Finance Items not Part of the Net cost of operations		
Change in budgetary resources obligated for goods, services and benefits ordered but not yet provided	(1,738,479)	(1,524,122)
Resources that fund expenses recognized in prior periods	(1,061,910)	(968,323)
Resources that finance the acquisition of assets	(865,725)	(733,311)
Total resources used to finance items not part of the net cost of operations	**(3,666,114)**	**(3,225,756)**
Total resources used to finance the net cost of operations	**$94,648,420**	**$90,518,020**
Components of the Net Cost of Operations that will not require or generate Resources in the Current Period		
Other	76,349	187,978
Depreciation and Amortization	1,716,058	1,589,059
Revaluation of assets or liabilities	-	113,113
Total components of Net Cost of Operations that will not require or generate resources in the current period	**1,792,407**	**1,890,150**
Net Cost of Operations	**$96,440,827**	**$92,408,170**

For Additional Information Contact:

Steven Goldberg
Chief Financial Officer
National Transportation Safety Board
Washington, DC 20594

cfofeed@ntsb.gov